The MIGHTY Accordion

The Complete Guide to Mastering Left Hand Bass/Chord Patterns

by David DiGiuseppe

A comprehensive collection of progressive exercises for playing bass/chord patterns on the 120 bass accordion. For beginners through advanced players.

Online Audio www.melbay.com/20740BCDEB

Audio Contents

audio #1

1	Exercise 2.1
2	Exercise 2.2
3	Exercise 2.3
4	Exercise 2.4
5	Exercise 2.5
6	Exercise 2.6
7	Exercise 2.7
8	Exercise 2.8
9	Exercise 2.9
10	Exercise 2.10
11	Exercise 2.11
12	Exercise 2.12
13	Exercise 2.13
14	Exercise 2.14
15	Exercise 2.15
16	Exercise 2.16
17	Exercise 2.17
18	Exercise 2.18
19	Exercise 2.19

20	Exercise 3.1
21	Exercise 3.2
22	Exercise 3.3
23	Exercise 3.4
24	Exercise 3.5
25	Exercise 3.6
26	Exercise 3.7
27	Exercise 3.8
28	Exercise 3.9
29	Exercise 3.10
30	Exercise 3.11
31	Exercise 3.12
32	Exercise 3.13
33	Exercise 3.14
34	Exercise 3.15
35	Exercise 3.16
36	Exercise 3.17
37	Exercise 4.1
38	Exercise 4.2

39	Exercise 4.3
40	Exercise 4.4
41	Exercise 4.5
42	Exercise 4.6
43	Exercise 4.7
44	Exercise 4.8
45	Exercise 4.9
46	Exercise 4.10

audio #2

1	Exercise 5.1
2	Exercise 5.2
3	Exercise 5.3
4	Exercise 5.4
5	Exercise 5.5
6	Exercise 5.6
7	Exercise 5.7
8	Exercise 5.8
9	Exercise 6.1

10	Exercise 6.2
11	Exercise 6.3
12	Exercise 6.4
13	Exercise 6.5
14	Exercise 6.6
15	Exercise 6.7
16	Exercise 6.8
17	Exercise 6.9
18	Exercise 6.10
19	Exercise 6.11
20	Exercise 6.12
21	Exercise 6.13
22	Exercise 6.14
23	Exercise 6.15
24	Exercise 6.16
25	Exercise 6.17
26	Exercise 6.18
27	Exercise 6.19
28	Exercise 6.20

29	Exercise 7.1
30	Exercise 7.2
31	Exercise 7.3
32	Exercise 7.4
33	Exercise 7.5
34	Exercise 7.6
35	Exercise 7.7
36	Exercise 7.8
37	Exercise 7.9
38	Exercise 7.10
39	Exercise 7.11
40	Exercise 7.12
41	Exercise 7.13
42	Exercise 7.14
43	Exercise 7.15
44	Exercise 7.16
45	Exercise 7.17
46	Exercise 7.18
47	Exercise 7.19

Cover photo ©Stockbyte.

1 2 3 4 5 6 7 8 9 0

Visit us on the Web at www.melbay.com — E-mail us at email@melbay.com

Contents

Introduction   A Note From the Author 4
     What This Book Offers   4
     Who Should Use This Book   5
     How To Use This Book   5
     About the CD   5
     Acknowledgements   5
   About the Author   6

Prelude   Music Notation 101 7
     Overview   7
     Staves and Notes   7
     The Treble and Bass Clefs   7
     Time Values   8
     Time Signature   9

Chapter 1   The Keyboard 11
     Notes on the Keyboard   11
   The Bass System
     Stradella and Free Bass Systems   11
     Stradella Bass Layout   12
     12 Bass Accordions   13
     The Accordion's Bass Notation   13
   Fingerings
     Fourth Finger on Root Method   15
     Third Finger on Root Method   16
     Left Hand Placement   16
   Basic Music Theory
     Sharps, Flats and Natural Signs   17
     Half Step and Whole Step Intervals   17
     Scales   17
     Key Signatures   18

Chapter 2   Getting Started 19
     Introducing C   19
     Introducing G   20
     Playing C and G   20
     Introducing F   21
     Playing F and C   21
     Playing F, C and G   22
   Basic Music Theory
     Intervals   23
   Congruous Chords and Longer Leaps
     Introducing D   26
     Playing F, C, G and D   27
     Introducing A   28
     Playing F, C, G, D and A   29
   Basic Music Theory
     Triads and Chords   32

Chapter 3   Alternating Bass Patterns 33
     Introducing the Alternate Bass   33
     Introducing Bb   34
     Introducing Eb   36
     Introducing E   36
   More Fun with Alternating Basses
     Alternate Bass Exercises   37
   Basic Music Theory
     Ties   42
     Accidentals   42

Chapter 4   Minor Chords 43
        Introducing the Minor Chord 43
        The Minor Chord with Alternating Bass 45
    More Fun with Minor Chords
        Minor Chord Challenges 47
Chapter 5   Seventh Chords 49
        Introducing the Seventh Chord 49
        The Seventh Chord with Alternating Bass 51
    Basic Music Theory
        Seventh Chords 53
Chapter 6   The Counter Bass 55
        Introducing the Counter Bass 55
        Linear Bass Lines 57
        Using the Fifth Finger 58
        Playing the Third with a Minor Chord 59
        An Alternative Fingering 60
        Linear Bass Lines with Minor Chords 60
Chapter 7   Diminished Chords 63
        Introducing the Diminished Chord 63
        The Diminished Chord with Alternating Bass 65
        The Diminished Chord with Linear Bass Lines 67
        The Diminished Chord with the Sixth 69
    Basic Music Theory
        Diminished Chords 70
    The Half Diminished Chord 71

Advanced Techniques – Chord Combinations

Chapter 8   Dominant, Major and Minor Seven Chords 75
        Overview 75
        One Button—Three Notes 75
        Notating Chord Combinations 75
        The Full Dominant Seven Chord 76
        The Minor Seven Chord 80
        The Major Seven Chord 84
    Basic Music Theory
        Chord Nomenclature 86
Chapter 9   The m7(b5) – 7(b9) Progression 87
        The 7(b9) Chord 87
        The m7(b5) Chord 91
        Special Note—The m7(b5) and m6 Chords 92
Chapter 10   The Major and Minor Six Chords 95
        Introducing the Major Six Chord 95
        Introducing the Minor Six Chord 97
Chapter 11   Major, Dominant and Minor Nine Chords 101
        Introducing the Major Nine Chord 101
        The Dominant Nine Chord 103
        The Minor Nine Chord 106
Chapter 12   The Leftovers...109
        The Augmented Triad 109
        The Six/Nine Chord 109
        The Minor Major Seven Chord 111
        The Suspended Four Chord 112

A Note From the Author

Ah, the accordion. A musical icon of the industrial age. A tour-de-force in the first half of the twentieth century. An instrument in search of a contemporary identity.

Its humble beginning was in Vienna, Austria, in 1829, where inventor Cyrill Demian presented a patent for a new instrument—the accordion.

Fast forward about three decades to Castelfidardo, Italy, where a farm hand named Paolo Soprani acquired an accordion. Combining an inquisitive mind, an innate gift for tinkering and a skill for hawking his wares, Soprani became a Henry Ford of the accordion. The seeds for the manufacturing of this instrument were sown and within a few more decades, a full harvest was reaped.

Perhaps the first mass produced instrument to conquer the world, some form of the "squeeze box" (keyboard accordion, button box, bandoneon, bayan, etc.) is now found in all regions of the world. By the 1950s almost half a million accordions per year were being manufactured in Italy and Germany—many of them arriving in the United States.

But times change, and by the late 1960s new trends in Western popular music had left the accordion wilting in the cold. The accordion's century–long rise in popularity was coming to an end. And with it came a significant decrease in the number of compositions, technical studies, "how to" books and manuscripts written specifically for the accordion.

The Mighty Accordion is my humble attempt at bridging this half–century gap.

What This Book Offers

The Mighty Accordion presents a series of exercises designed to progressively enhance playing the left hand of an accordion with the standard Stradella 120 bass system. The first few chapters assume little or no knowledge of—or experience with—the instrument. The exercises slowly and methodically increase in difficulty as new concepts are introduced.

Chapters one through seven begin with exercises playing simple bass/chord patterns. A systematic introduction of additional techniques and challenges ensues, ultimately integrating major, minor, seventh and diminished buttons, bass patterns and chord progressions.

Chapters eight through twelve present exercises designed to facilitate the use and understanding of button combinations needed to play chords which cannot be voiced with only a single button. This advanced section will be especially useful for those playing jazz tunes.

Throughout this book, explanations are offered on the workings of the instrument, the mechanics and relevance of each newly introduced concept, and of pertinent music theory. A short narrative precedes each exercise and highlights its salient features and challenges.

This manual focuses exclusively on playing bass/chord patterns with the bass side of the accordion. The use of single bass note passages and solos, although essential to good musicianship, is not covered in this book. Also entirely omitted is the use of the accordion's keyboard side, whether playing melody or chords.

Who Should Use This Book
This guide is intended for anyone who wishes to improve their skills in playing the accordion's bass side. The studies and techniques start simply but end with advanced concepts, offering a wealth of material to the beginner as well as the proficient accordionist.

How To Use This Book
It is not essential to start with the beginning exercises in this collection. Given the progressive nature of these studies, identify the exercises which are at the edge of your abilities and start there. You may, however, find it useful to review chapter one to become familiar with the notation convention used in this book.

Each exercise should be played slowly and accurately from the start. As your playing of the study improves, the tempo can be increased. *Play each exercise no faster than you can play it well. It is a waste of valuable time to practice your mistakes!*

About the CDs
Every exercise in chapters 1 through 7 can be heard on the accompanying CDs. Disc and track numbers are indicated next to the corresponding exercise number in the book. On each track, the exercise is played at two tempos. It is first played slowly. The exercise is then repeated at a moderate speed.

Acknowledgements
I offer heartfelt thanks to the following individuals for their comments, advice and insights: Melanie Climis, Bob Haddad, Dean Herington, Anita Carroll-Weldon, Robbie Link, Tony Galfano and Phil Marsosudiro. And a special thanks goes out to my wife Nina. Without her invaluable suggestions and unending support, this project would not have been possible.

About the Author

David DiGiuseppe has been performing professionally since 1978. Appearing solo or with his numerous bands, he is known for his fiery and emotive playing. He is equally at home playing Irish tunes in a pub, French musettes in a cabaret, contra or Cajun music for a dance, or performing in the intimate setting of a concert hall.

DiGiuseppe's musical career began at the tender age of three in a local barber shop, where he was often lifted onto a chair and encouraged to sing his favorite songs. At the impressionable age of eight, he was taking accordion lessons at Petteruti's School of Music in Providence, Rhode Island. When he was twelve, he put his accordion in the closet and began playing Beatles' tunes on the guitar. In 1984, DiGiuseppe "rediscovered" his accordion and has since become an accomplished player and instructor.

DiGiuseppe is featured on a number of recordings. *Movin' On* highlights his ever–fiery accordion fronting a lively collection of spirited jigs, driving reels and beautiful waltzes. *Welcome to Heaven...* showcases his extraordinary playing on music from Celtic, Parisian and American traditions. Reviewer John O'Regan of Ireland wrote, "...a player of immense talent and vision, David is a musician worth encountering." Mary DesRosiers in *Sing Out!* wrote "There is a wide and stunning array of music represented here...DiGiuseppe handles them all deftly."

His first solo recording—*South of Andromeda*—featuring traditional songs, dance tunes and original compositions, has been hailed as "a justification for the right to life of the humble accordion when squeezed by the right hands." *(Victory Review)* DiGiuseppe is featured on four releases by his band FootLoose and appears on numerous CDs backing other musicians.

DiGiuseppe has previously published two books with Mel Bay Publications. *100 Tunes for Piano Accordion* (MB97210) is an extensive collection of reels, jigs, hornpipes and polkas from the French Canadian, Cape Breton, Scottish, Shetland, New England and Southern Old Time Traditions. *100 Irish Tunes for Piano Accordion* (MB97211CD) is a collection of traditional Irish jigs, reels and hornpipes arranged for the accordion.

Find out more about David DiGiuseppe at www.DavidDG.com.

Music Notation 101

Overview

This chapter offers a basic introduction to the music notation which will be used throughout this book. If you already know how to read music, feel free to skip ahead to Chapter One.

It is beyond the scope and intention of this section to offer a complete course on music notation and theory. Those desiring a more thorough explanation of the following concepts should seek additional text or course work. Included here is a brief introduction to music fundamentals.

Staves and Notes

Written music is notated on five parallel lines called a STAFF (see *Illustration P.1*).

Illustration P.1 – a staff made of five lines and four spaces

NOTES are placed on the staff to convey two important pieces of information—pitch and duration. The duration or length of time a note is played is indicated by its shape. (See Time Values section on the next page for details.)

The pitch (how high or low a tone sounds) is indicated by placing the note on a LINE of the staff or in the SPACE between two lines (see *Illustration P.2*). The note placement correlates to pitch—the higher the note appears on the staff, the higher it is in pitch.

Illustration P.2 – various notes on a staff

The Treble and Bass Clefs

Each line and space on a staff has a name taken from the first seven letters of the alphabet—A through G. A CLEF is placed at the beginning of each staff designating which lines and spaces represent which note names. There are two clefs used in accordion music:

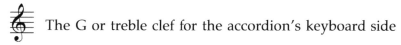
The G or treble clef for the accordion's keyboard side

The F or bass clef for the accordion's bass side

Illustration P.3 on the following page shows the names of the notes on a staff with a treble or G clef. Notice that the names follow the alphabet sequentially, going from low to high in both pitch and location on the staff.

C E G B D F A D F A C E G

C D E F G A B C D E F G A

Illustration P.3 – names of the notes on the lines and spaces
of a staff with a treble clef

The accordion's bass side is notated in the F or bass clef. *Illustration P.4* shows the notes on a staff written in the bass clef. Notice that the names of the lines are different from those of the treble clef. For example, the first line of the bass clef is the note G, while the first line is the note E on the treble clef.

C E G B D F A D F A C E G

C D E F G A B C D E F G A B C D

Illustration P.4 – names of the notes on the lines and spaces
of a staff with a bass clef

Time Values

As previously mentioned, the second piece of information represented by a note on a staff is its duration or time value. The time value (how long a note is played) is conveyed by the note's appearance. *Illustration P.5* shows the time values of commonly played notes.

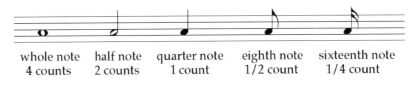

whole note   half note   quarter note   eighth note   sixteenth note
4 counts   2 counts   1 count   1/2 count   1/4 count

Illustration P.5 – time values of various notes

Note values are all relative. *Illustration P.6* shows that a half note, which gets two counts, is half the value of a whole note, which gets four counts. A quarter note (one count) is half the value of a half note, and an eighth note (one half count) is half the value of a quarter note. A sixteenth note is half the value of an eighth note.

whole note = 2 half notes = 4 quarter notes = 8 eighth notes = 16 sixteenth notes

Illustration P.6 – the relative value of notes

A dot placed next to a note adds half of the note's value to the original note, as shown in *Illustration P.7*. A dotted half note gets three counts—two for the half note plus one (half of a half note). A dotted quarter note gets one and a half counts.

dotted half note = half note + quarter note   dotted quarter note = quarter note + eighth note

Illustration P.7 – dotted notes

Time Signature

A MEASURE is the basic building block of a musical composition's rhythm. Each measure is bounded by vertical lines crossing the staff called BAR LINES (*see Illustration P.8*). A measure can have any number of counts, though two, three, four and six counts are the most common in western music.

A TIME SIGNATURE is found at the beginning of each piece of written music. The time signature conveys two pieces of information—how many counts are in each measure and which note gets one count.

The top digit of the time signature indicates the number of counts or beats in each measure. This number of counts will recur in every measure of a piece, or until another time signature is encountered.

The lower digit of the time signature indicates which note gets one count. Typically, but not always, the quarter note gets one count, which is indicated by a 4 shown as the lower number. If an eighth note is to get one count, an 8 will be placed in the lower position of the time signature. Likewise, if a half note is to get one beat, the lower number will be a 2.

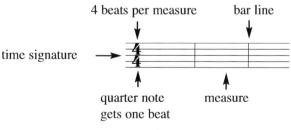

Illustration P.8

The time signature $\frac{4}{4}$ is also referred to as COMMON TIME, indicated with a **C**.

 is the same as C

Remember, note values are relative. If the time signature indicates that an eighth note gets one count, then a quarter note will get two counts, a half note four counts, etc. Notice that the relative time values of the notes stay the same.

In the time signature shown in *Illustration P.9*, there are three beats per measure while the eighth note gets one beat. Notice that the first measure contains three eighth notes, while the second measure contains a dotted quarter note. Both measures contain three beats.

Illustration P.9 – three beats per measure,
the eighth note gets one beat

In *Illustration P.10*, there are six beats per measure while the eighth note gets one beat.

Illustration P.10 – six beats per measure,
the eighth note gets one beat

The time signature of *Illustration P.11* shows two beats per measure. The 2 placed in the lower position indicates that a half note gets one count. Again, with all notes being relative, a whole note gets two counts.

Illustration P.11 – two beats per measure,
the half note gets one beat

$\frac{2}{2}$ is often referred to as CUT COMMON TIME, which is indicated with a $\mathcal{C}$.

$\frac{2}{2}$ is the same as $\mathcal{C}$

The Keyboard

Notes on the Keyboard

The notes of the keyboard side of the accordion are written in the G or treble clef. *Illustration 1.1* shows an accordion keyboard and its related notes on a staff.

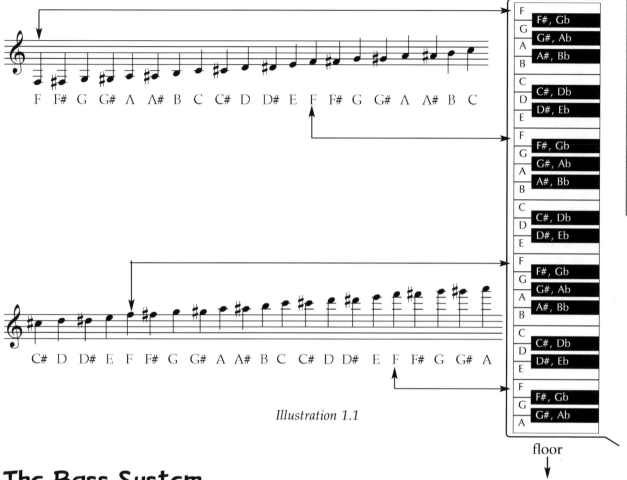

Chapter 1

Illustration 1.1

The Bass System

Stradella and Free Bass Systems

There are currently two types of accordion bass systems in common use, the Stradella and the free bass. The Stradella system, comprised of single notes and chords, is the most frequently found system for piano accordions in the United States. The number of bass buttons available ranges from 12 to 120, with 120 being the most common.

In the free bass system, each button plays an individual note, offering more flexibility and variety but presenting more of a challenge. There are various free bass systems with differing note patterns, including Western Bassetti, the Quint free bass and the Russian Bayan free bass systems.

Some accordions have both systems, with a converter arrangement that allows the player to switch between the free bass and Stradella systems.

This book describes the Stradella system only.

Stradella Bass Layout

Although the accordion left hand or bass side may at first appear to be an overwhelming collection of buttons, the Stradella system is in fact quite logically laid out and consequently, it is easy to understand and master.

Pressing a button on the bass side plays either a single note or a chord (three notes sounded together). *Illustration 1.2* shows the names of the notes and chords. Chords are indicated by the use of M (major), m (minor), 7 (seventh) or d (diminished) after the note name.

Notice that the buttons in the two inner columns are individual notes, while the buttons in the other four columns are chords.

A chord is simply a grouping of specific notes. Each accordion chord button plays three notes simultaneously.

For example, the CM button plays a C major chord by sounding the notes C, E and G at the same time. A detailed discussion of chords will be found later in this book.

Also notice that the E, C and Ab buttons in the second inner column are shaded. On most accordions these three buttons are physically indented to assist in locating them.

See page 17 for an explanation of sharps (#) and flats (b).

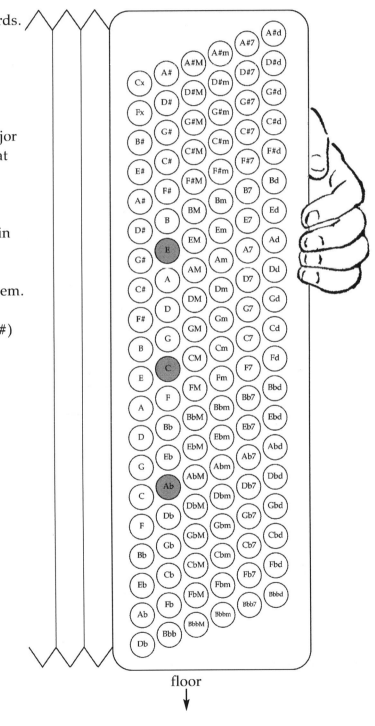

*Illustration 1.2 – notes and chords
of the Stradella 120 bass system*

floor

12

12 Bass Accordions

Beginner's accordions typically have 12 bass buttons. *Illustration 1.3* shows the note arrangement of a 12 bass accordion. Notice that the C bass note is physically indented as a reference.

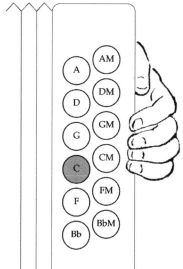

Illustration 1.3 – notes and chords of the Stradella 12 bass system

The Accordion's Bass Notation

Music written for the accordion has its own convention to convey which note or chord on the bass side is to be played. The staff corresponding to the accordion's bass is written in the bass clef. Notes written on or below the third staff line with the stem up are single bass notes, as shown in *Illustration 1.4*.

Illustration 1.4 – single bass notes

Notes written above the third line with the stem down represent chords, as shown in *Illustration 1.5*.

Illustration 1.5 – chords

To distinguish between different types of chords, a letter is place above the note: M for major chord, m for minor chord, 7 for seventh chord, and d for diminished chord, as shown in *Illustration 1.6* (also refer to *Illustration 1.2* on page 12).

The inner two columns of a 120 button accordion are all single bass notes, while the remaining four play chords. Each chord column includes only one type of chord. For instance, the third column plays only major chords, while the fourth column plays only minor chords.

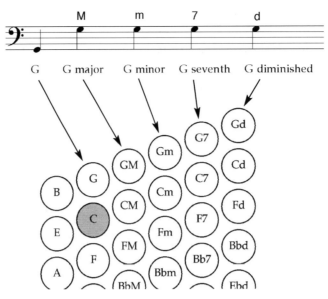

Illustration 1.6 – bass, major, minor, seventh and
diminished columns and their staff notation

The first column is referred to as the COUNTER BASS column, while the second one is called the FUNDAMENTAL. To indicate use of the counter bass, a line is drawn under the note, as shown in *Illustration 1.7*. Notice that the counter bass E is the same note as fundamental E, though it is played with a different button.

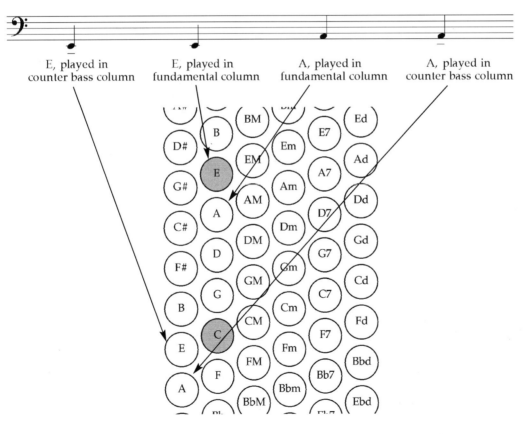

Illustration 1.7 – bass (fundamental) and counter bass notation

Fingerings

There are two schools of thought regarding fingering for the bass side of the accordion.

Fourth Finger on Root Method

This fingering convention uses the fourth (ring) finger to play the fundamental and counter bass columns, with the second and third fingers playing the chords and notes of that row.

    1a) When playing a pattern with the fundamental and major chord (*see Illustration 1.8*):

        4th finger on fundamental or counter bass columns

        3rd finger on major chord

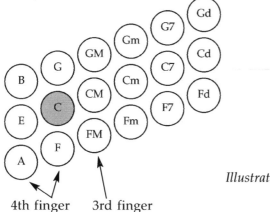

Illustration 1.8 – fingering

For example, place your fourth finger on the C button in the fundamental column and place your third finger on the CM chord button. Your fingers are now in the C major position. In this case, the note C is also called the ROOT of the chord.

    1b) For playing fundamental and minor, seventh or diminished chord (*see Illustration 1.9*):

        4th finger on bass or counter bass (use with seventh chords only)

        2nd finger on minor, seventh or diminished chord

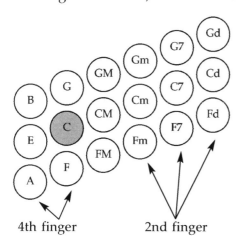

Illustration 1.9 – fingering

Third Finger on Root Method

This method uses the third (middle) finger to play the root of the chord (in the fundamental column), with the second finger playing the major or minor chord. When playing a pattern using the seventh or diminished chords, the fourth finger is placed in the fundamental column, with the second finger playing the seventh or diminished chord.

2a) When playing a bass pattern with root (fundamental) and major or minor chord:

3rd finger on fundamental or counter bass (use with major chord only)

2nd finger on major chord or minor chord

2b) When playing a pattern with root and seventh or diminished chord:

4th finger on root or counter bass column (use with seventh chords only)

2nd finger on seventh or diminished

This author has a strong preference for the first system. Consequently, all suggested fingerings given in this book will be consistent with Fourth Finger on Root method.

Left Hand Placement

When playing the accordion, the left hand is placed through the bass strap. Your hand must be positioned far enough through the strap such that all the buttons (including the counter bass row) can easily be reached, but not so far through that the hand is cramped when reaching for a note. Typically, the left hand strap is positioned where your wrist watch would normally be.

The tension of the bass strap can be adjusted by turning the wheel sitting above the strap on top of the accordion. (Note that some lower–priced accordions do not have this adjustment.) The strap should be adjusted such that it is just loose enough for your hand to move freely up and down, without much extra play. Your left hand fingers should be curled, so that any button can be depressed with the finger tip. At all times, your hand and fingers must stay relaxed. *Illustration 1.10* shows the left hand placement.

Illustration 1.10

Basic Music Theory

Sharps, b Flats and ♮ Natural Signs

Look at an accordion keyboard and you'll notice white keys and black keys in a repeating pattern. The white keys are called the NATURAL NOTES while the black keys are the SHARPS and FLATS.

A SHARP SIGN (#) placed in front of a note on a staff raises that note by one half step—to the adjacent note with a higher pitch.

A FLAT SIGN (b) placed in front of a note on a staff lowers that note by one half step—to the adjacent note with a lower pitch.

A NATURAL SIGN (♮) placed in front of a note cancels a sharp or flat.

Notice that C# and Db are the same key—and pitch—on the keyboard, but are different notes on the staff. Also notice that E# is the same key as F and that B natural and Cb are the same keys. Two notes of the same pitch with different names are said to be ENHARMONIC EQUIVALENTS.

Half Step and Whole Step Intervals

An INTERVAL is defined as the difference in pitch between two notes. The smallest interval in Western music is the HALF STEP—the distance between any two adjacent notes. On a keyboard, examples of half step intervals are C to C# and C# to D. Notice that E to F and B to C are also half step intervals, as there are no black keys (sharps or flats) between them.

The interval made of two adjacent half steps is called a WHOLE STEP. Examples of whole step intervals include C to D, A to B, and E to F#.

Scales

A SCALE is a defined pattern of whole and half steps. One common scale in Western music is the MAJOR SCALE. A major scale is made by starting on any note and following the pattern of: whole step, whole step, half step, whole step, whole step, whole step, half step. The following page shows a major scale starting with the note C.

Notice that the C major scale consists of all natural notes, that is, there are no sharps or flats in the scale. Consequently, the key of C is also referred to "the natural scale".

Now let's create a major scale starting on the note D. Following the major scale pattern of whole and half steps, we end up with:

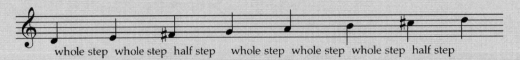

whole step   whole step   half step   whole step   whole step   whole step   half step

Notice that F# and C# are needed to maintain the correct pattern of whole and half steps. We therefore say that the KEY SIGNATURE of D Major has two sharps, F# and C#. Hence, music written in the key of D shows the following key signature:

If we start with the note F and apply the major scale whole/half pattern, we'll end up with a Bb in the key signature. Therefore, the key signature of F major is Bb, as shown below.

The key signature is always shown at the beginning of each line of music, placed after the clef.

Key Signatures

Creating a major scale (by following the prescribed set of whole and half steps) from any individual note will create a unique key signature. Here is a list of the major keys and their key signatures.

C major	no sharps or flats		
G major	F#	F major	Bb
D major	F#, C#	Bb major	Bb, Eb
A major	F#, C#, G#	Eb major	Bb, Eb, Ab
E major	F#, C#, G#, D#	Ab major	Bb, Eb, Ab, Db
B major	F#, C#, G#, D#, A#	Db major	Bb, Eb, Ab, Db, Gb
F# major	F#, C#, G#, D#, A#, E#	Gb major	Bb, Eb, Ab, Db, Gb, Cb
C# Major	F#, C#, G#, D#, A#, E#, B#	Cb major	Bb, Eb, Ab, Db, Gb, Cb, Fb

Getting Started

Chapter 2

Introducing C

Let's start by playing two buttons on the accordion's bass side, the C bass note and the C major chord. *Illustration 2.1* shows where the buttons are found (also refer to *Illustration 1.2* on page 12). Notice that the C bass button is physically indented to assist in its identification.

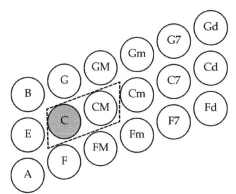

Illustration 2.1 – C bass and C major buttons

C bass is played with the fourth finger, while C major is played with the third. When playing, keep your fingers curled and relaxed (see *Illustration 1.10*), pressing each note with the fingertip. Press with a firm but relaxed attack. It is imperative to train your fingers to stay close to the buttons, even when not pressing them. Do not allow your fingers to rise away uncontrolled from the buttons when not in use.

In *Exercise 2.1*, the time signature indicates there are three counts per measure and the quarter note gets one count. Say 1–2–3 evenly and slowly for each measure, and play one note on each count. The double bar with two dots at the end of the line is a REPEAT SIGN, indicating the line is repeated from the beginning. The numbers below the first two notes indicate which fingers are to be used. The M indicates use of the major chord button and appears each time a new chord is to be played.

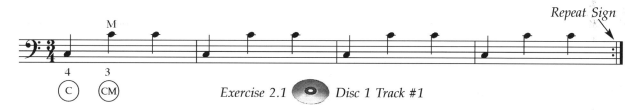

Exercise 2.1 Disc 1 Track #1

In *Exercise 2.2* play C and C major again, but notice there are four beats per measure. Count 1–2–3–4 evenly for each measure and play one note per count.

Exercise 2.2 Disc 1 Track #2

Repeat *Exercises 2.1* and *2.2*, playing slowly and accurately. It may take many repetitions to develop the control necessary to play the lines properly.

Introducing G

Exercise 2.3 and *Exercise 2.4* introduce the G bass note and the G major chord. *Illustration 2.2* shows where these buttons are found (also refer to *Illustration 1.2* on page 12). Notice the notes lie directly above C and C major. As in the C position, use the fourth and third fingers to play G and G major.

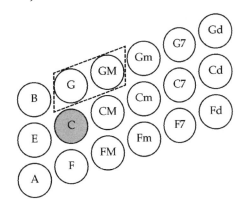

Illustration 2.2 – G and G major buttons

Exercise 2.3   Disc 1 Track #3

Notice that in *Exercise 2.4* there are four counts or beats per measure.

Exercise 2.4   Disc 1 Track #4

Playing C and G

Exercises 2.5 and *2.6* move between the C and the G rows. Notice that the correct fingering calls for the fourth and third fingers on the C row, which are then moved to the G position. Play slowly and accurately. Again, it may take many repetitions to play the line properly.

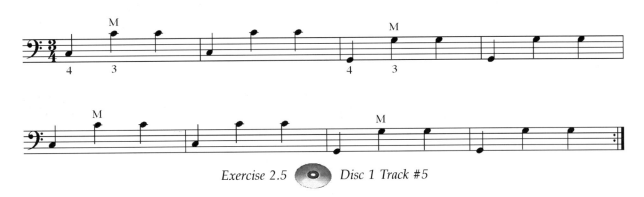

Exercise 2.5   Disc 1 Track #5

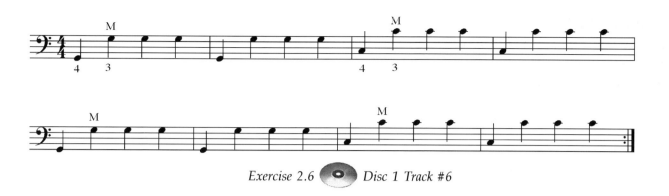

Exercise 2.6 💿 *Disc 1 Track #6*

Introducing F

Exercise 2.7 introduces the F bass note and the F major chord. *Illustration 2.3* shows where the buttons are found (also refer to *Illustration 1.2* on page 12). Notice the buttons lie directly below C and C major.

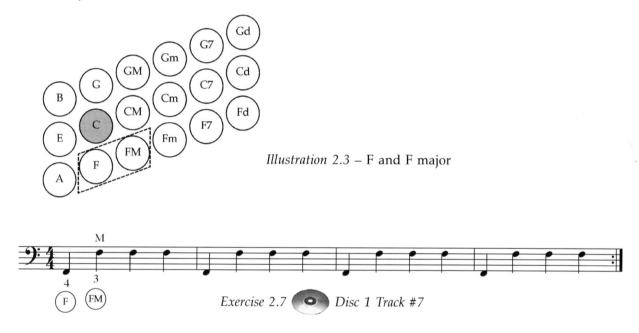

Illustration 2.3 – F and F major

Exercise 2.7 💿 *Disc 1 Track #7*

Playing F and C

In *Exercise 2.8*, play the notes of the F and C rows. Notice in measure 9 the F and F major buttons are played together for the full three beats of the measure. Remember to use the correct fingering.

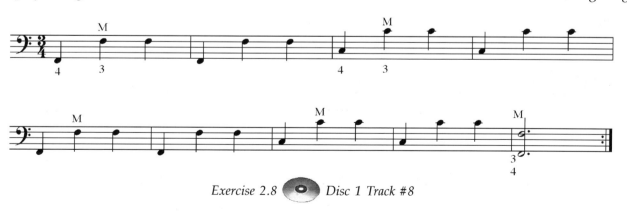

Exercise 2.8 💿 *Disc 1 Track #8*

Playing F, C and G

Exercises 2.9 and *2.10* move between the F, C and G rows. Practice slowly at first. Learn to jump accurately from F to G.

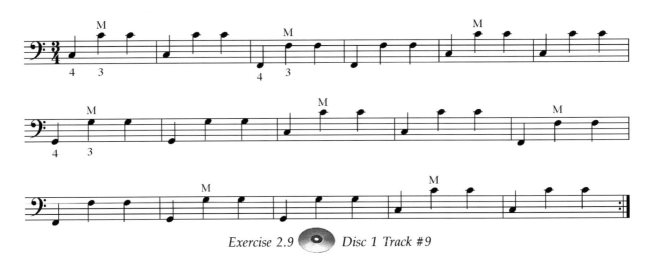

Exercise 2.9   Disc 1 Track #9

The first note of *Exercise 2.10* is C, but is located on the staff an octave below the C at the start of *Exercise 2.9*. Although written differently, they are played with the same C bass button and, therefore, sound the same.

Exercise 2.10   Disc 1 Track #10

Review all the exercises presented thus far until you can play them easily. It is important to be able to play these exercises well before moving on to the more complicated ones.

Intervals

When working with chords, it is useful to understand the concept of INTERVALS. An interval is defined as the difference in pitch between two notes. The smallest interval in western music is the half step (see page 17). The interval made of two adjacent half steps is called a whole step.

Intervals are defined by two terms, one QUALITATIVE and one QUANTITATIVE. The quantitative term counts the letter names between the two notes. For example, C to D is a second, C to E is a third. To identify this quantitative term, simply count the names of each note in the scale between the lower and upper. Be sure to count the lower note as 1. So for example, the interval between G and C is a fourth—G, A, B, C. The example below illustrates the intervals above the G note.

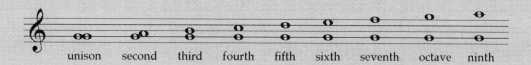

unison   second   third   fourth   fifth   sixth   seventh   octave   ninth

Notice the first interval in the example above is called a UNISON, which describes the interval between two of the same notes. Also notice that the term OCTAVE is used to describe the interval of an eighth.

These quantitative terms describe intervals starting on any note. Hence G to A is a second, as is A to B and B to C. But notice that the distance from G to A and from A to B is a whole step, while the distance between B and C is only one half step (again, see page 17). It therefore becomes necessary to qualify the type of second to accurately describe the distance between the interval's two notes. Thus the quantitative term is preceded by a one word description of the interval's quality, which can be either PERFECT, MAJOR, MINOR, DIMINISHED or AUGMENTED. This is the case with every interval.

Major and perfect intervals are created when the top note of the interval falls within the major scale of the lower note. (See page 17 for a discussion of scales.) Intervals of the unison, fourth, fifth and octave are called perfect. Intervals of the second, third, sixth and seventh are called major.

For example, the interval between C and D is a second. Since D is a note in the C major scale, the interval is called a major second. The interval between C and E is a third. Since E is a note in the C major scale, the interval is called a major third. The interval between C and F is a fourth. Since F is a note in the C major scale, the interval is called a perfect fourth.

The term "perfect" relates to the similar physical properties of the sound waves of the unison, fourth, fifth and octave. It is beyond the scope of this book to explore this phenomenon.

The example below shows the perfect and major intervals above the notes C and E.

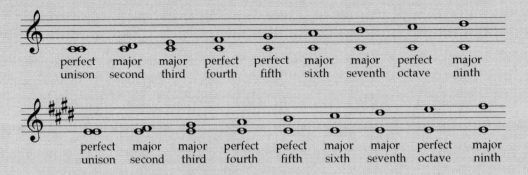

When a perfect interval is decreased in size by one half step, it becomes a diminished interval. For example, C to G is a perfect fifth. Lower the G by one half step to Gb, and the interval is called a diminished fifth. The example below shows the perfect and diminished intervals above the notes C and E.

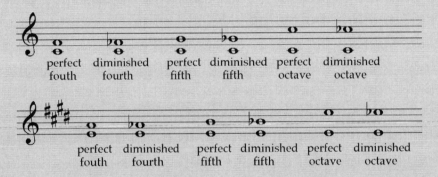

When a major interval is decreased in size by one half step it becomes a minor interval. For example, C to D is a major second, while C to Db is a minor second. The example below shows the major and minor intervals above the notes C and E.

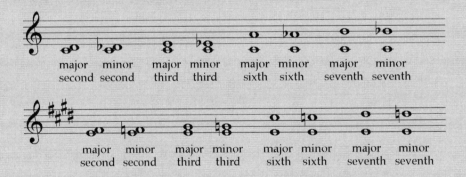

When a minor interval is decreased in size by one half step, it becomes a diminished interval. For example, C to E is a major third. Lowering the E by one half step results in the interval of C to Eb which is a minor third. Lowering the Eb by another half step—to Ebb—results in a diminished third (Ebb is the same note as D). A DOUBLE FLAT (bb) is used to indicate that a note is lowered by two half steps.

Notice in the above example the major interval has been decreased by a DOUBLE FLAT (bb), which is equivalent to lowering a note two half steps, which also equals one whole step. Shown below are examples of a major, minor and diminished third and seventh.

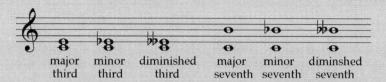

When a perfect or major interval is increased in size by one half step, it becomes an augmented interval. For example, C to F is a perfect fourth, while C to F# is an augmented fourth. C to A is a major sixth. C to A# is an augmented sixth.

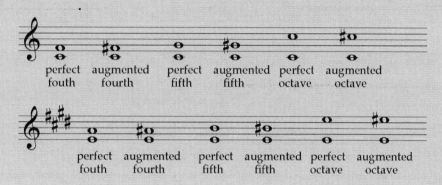

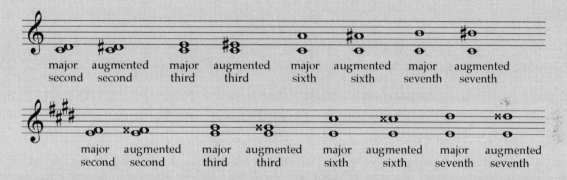

The symbol x used in the last line of the above example represents a DOUBLE SHARP. Notice the key signature of E major is F#, C#, G# and D#. The double sharp is used on the E augmented second to indicate that the F# is raised by a half step to become F##, or Fx. Likewise, E to G# is a major third, while E to Gx (##) is an augmented third.

Congruous Chords and Longer Leaps

Introducing D

Exercises 2.11 and *2.12* introduce the D bass note and the D major chord. *Illustration 2.4* shows where these buttons are found (also refer to *Illustration 1.2* on page 12). Notice the buttons lie directly above G and G major.

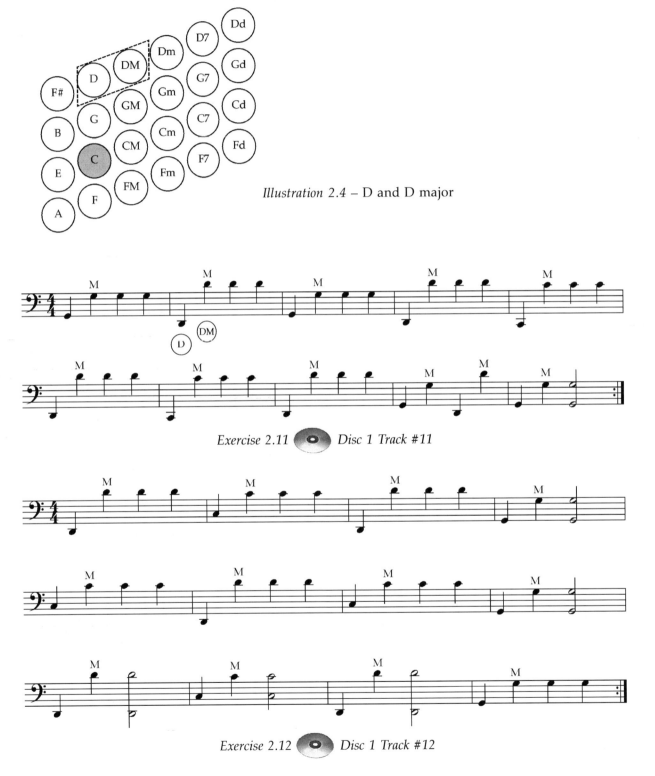

Illustration 2.4 – D and D major

Exercise 2.11   Disc 1 Track #11

Exercise 2.12   Disc 1 Track #12

26

Playing Γ, C, G and D

Exercises 2.13 and *2.14* use all the notes you've learned thus far. Practice slowly. It may take many repetitions to accurately make the jump from the F row to the D row.

Exercise 2.13   *Disc 1 Track #13*

Exercise 2.14   *Disc 1 Track #14*

Introducing A

Exercise 2.15 introduces the A bass note and the A major chord. *Illustration 2.5* shows where these buttons are found (also refer to *Illustration 1.2* on page 12). Notice the buttons lie directly above D and D major.

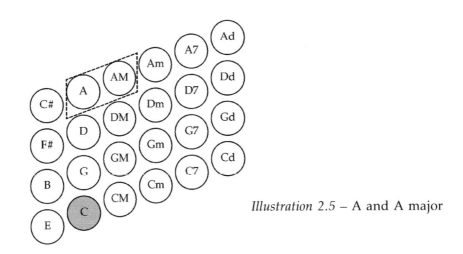

Illustration 2.5 – A and A major

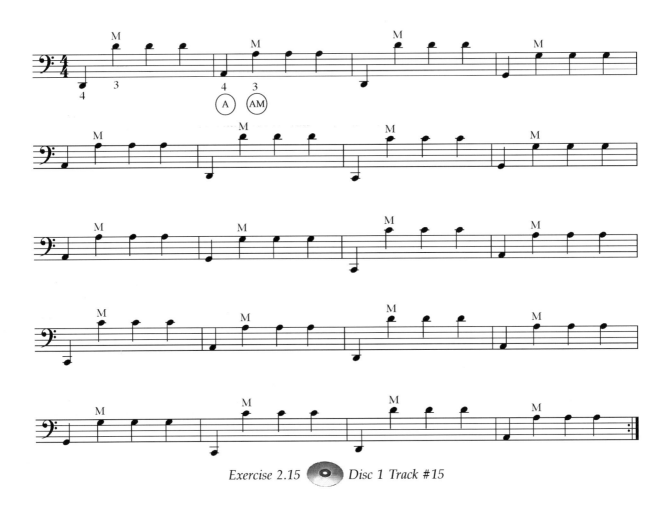

Exercise 2.15 *Disc 1 Track #15*

Playing F, C, G, D and A

Exercise 2.16 through *Exercise* 2.19 use all the notes you've learned thus far. A new pattern is introduced in *Exercise 2.16*. The bass note and chord buttons are played together for two beats each.

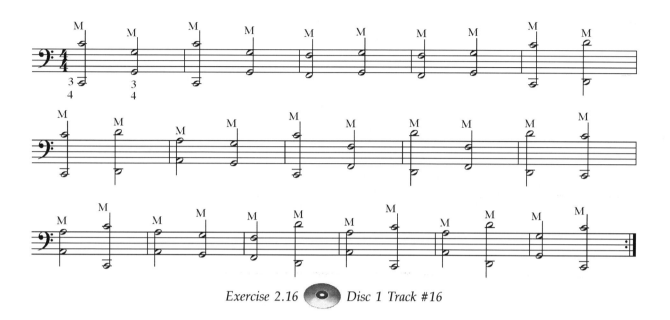

Exercise 2.16 💿 *Disc 1 Track #16*

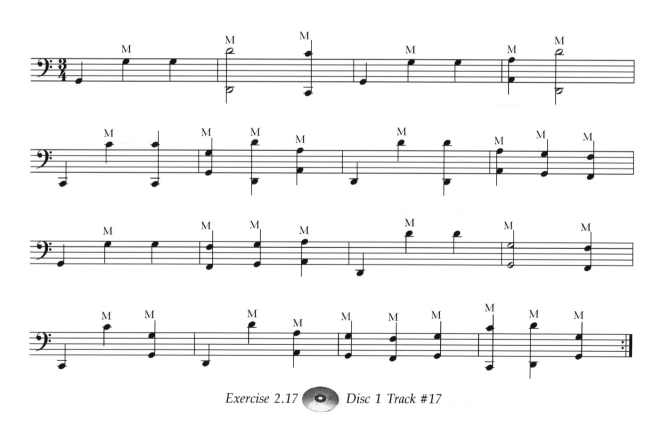

Exercise 2.17 💿 *Disc 1 Track #17*

Exercise 2.18 uses a pattern with the bass notes being played on beats one and four of each measure, and chords being played on beats two and three. Maintain the use of fingers four and three as you jump between chord positions.

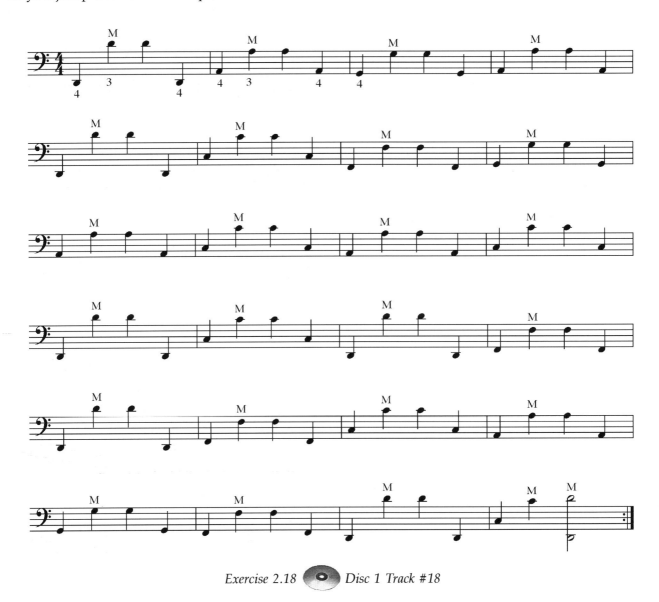

Exercise 2.18 Disc 1 Track #18

Exercise 2.19 will prove to be a challenge, with leaps between the F chord and A chord positions. Play slowly until you can play it accurately. As in the previous exercises, maintain the use of fingers four and three as you jump between chord positions. We will explore alternate fingerings later in this book.

Exercise 2.19 🔘 *Disc 1 Track #19*

Triads and Chords

A CHORD is defined as two or more notes sounding simultaneously. A TRIAD is a three note chord. A triad consists of the lowest note, called the ROOT or FUNDAMENTAL, plus notes a third and a fifth above the root.

A MAJOR TRIAD or MAJOR CHORD consists of the root and notes a major third and a perfect fifth above the root. For example, C to E is a major third, and C to G is a perfect fifth, so C, E and G make a C major chord. The example below illustrates the intervals making up the C major, D major and Eb major triads.

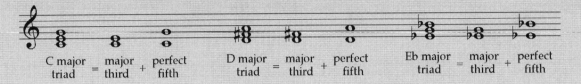

A MINOR TRIAD is made of a minor third and a perfect 5th. For example, C to Eb is a minor third, and C to G is a perfect fifth, so C, Eb and G make a C minor chord. Below are examples of the C minor, D minor and Eb minor triads.

An AUGMENTED TRIAD consists of a major third and an augmented 5th. The C augmented, D augmented and Eb augmented chords are shown below.

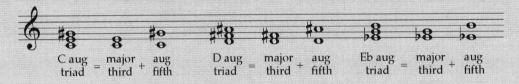

A DIMINISHED TRIAD consists of a minor third and a diminished 5th.

The basic and most commonly played chords contain 3 or 4 notes, which include the major chord, minor chord, dominant seventh chord, major seventh, minor seventh and diminished chord. We will explore these chords later in this book.

Alternating Bass Patterns

Introducing the Alternate Bass

A common pattern played on the accordion's bass side uses the ALTERNATE BASS played with the fundamental bass and chord. The alternate bass is the button above the fundamental. When playing the C bass and C major chord, the alternate bass is G (see *Illustration 3.1* below and *Illustration 1.2* on page 12).

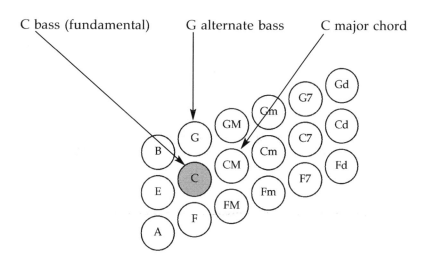

Illustration 3.1 – C position and G alternate bass

Illustration 3.2 shows the G bass and G major buttons with their alternate bass D.

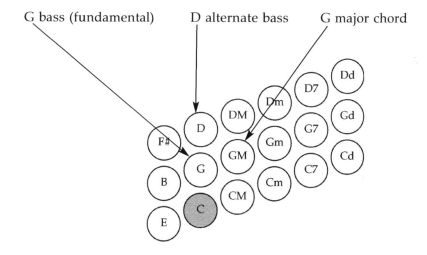

Illustration 3.2 – G position and D alternate bass

Exercise 3.1 shows the alternate bass pattern written on a staff with the suggested fingering. Notice that the alternate bass G is played with the second finger, maintaining the placement of fourth finger on the C bass and third finger on the C chord. Play slowly at first. Remember to keep your fingers close to the buttons when they are not playing a note, preventing them from flying uncontrolled away from the buttons.

Chapter 3

G alternate bass

Exercise 3.1 — *Disc 1 Track #20*

In *Exercise 3.2*, the C, G and F chord positions use the alternate bass.

Exercise 3.2 — *Disc 1 Track #21*

Introducing Bb

Exercise 3.3 introduces the Bb bass note and the Bb major chord. *Illustration 3.3* (also refer to *Illustration 1.2* on page 12) shows Bb lies below the F row. Notice the second measure of *Exercise 3.3* incorporates the use of the F alternate bass. The exercise is written in the key of F, with a key signature of Bb. Consequently, every note B in the exercise is played as a Bb. See pages 17 and 18 for a discussion of key signatures.

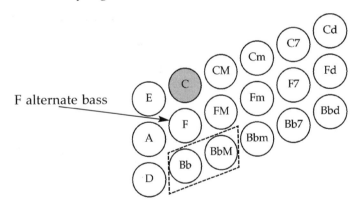

Illustration 3.3 – Bb and Bb major

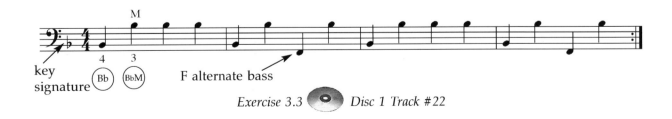

key signature   F alternate bass

Exercise 3.3 — *Disc 1 Track #22*

In *Exercise 3.4* and *Exercise 3.5* use the alternate bass pattern with correct fingering as you jump from one chord position to another.

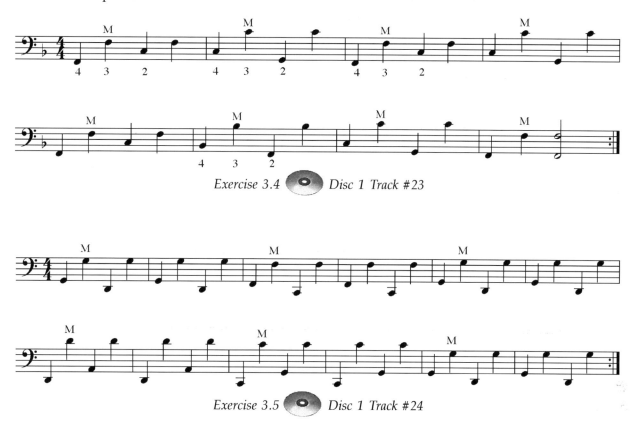

Exercise 3.4   Disc 1 Track #23

Exercise 3.5   Disc 1 Track #24

Exercise 3.6 uses the alternating bass pattern in 3/4 time. Notice that there are two chords played as quarter notes between each bass note.

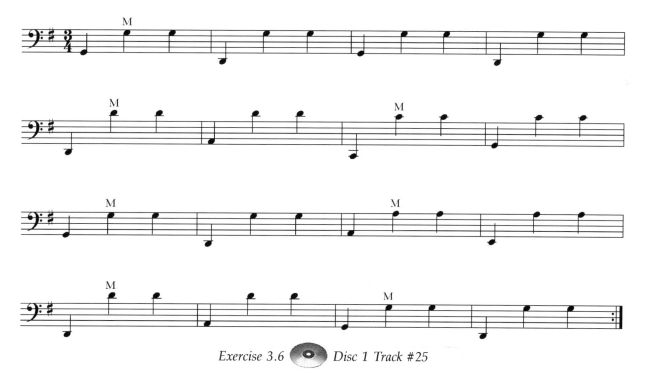

Exercise 3.6   Disc 1 Track #25

Introducing Eb

Exercise 3.7 and *Exercise 3.8* use the Eb bass note and the Eb major chord. *Illustration 3.4* (also refer to *Illustration 1.2* on page 12) shows that Eb lies below the Bb.

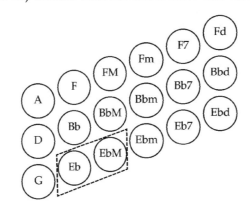

Illustration 3.4 – Eb and Eb major

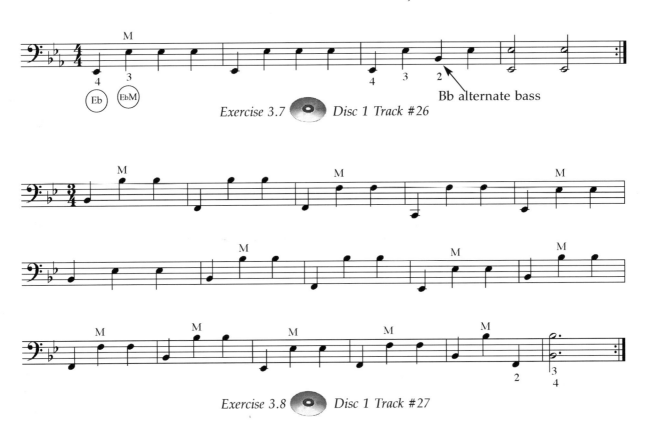

Exercise 3.7   Disc 1 Track #26

Exercise 3.8   Disc 1 Track #27

Introducing E

Exercise 3.9 introduces the E bass and E major. E lies above A as shown in *Illustration 3.5* (also refer to *Illustration 1.2* on page 12). On most accordions, the E bass button is physically marked with an indentation. Notice the difference in the key signatures of *Exercises 3.8* and *3.9*.

Exercise 3.9   Disc 1 Track #28

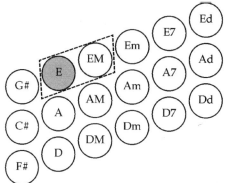

Illustration 3.5 – E and E major

Exercise 3.10 uses E as the alternate bass in measures 2 and 6, and a fundamental bass in measures 3, 7 and 9.

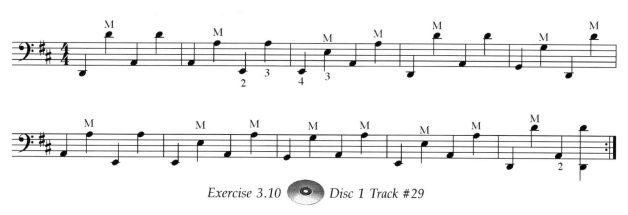

Exercise 3.10  *Disc 1 Track #29*

More Fun with Alternating Basses

Alternate Bass Exercises

Practice the following exercises carefully to develop facility in using the alternate bass pattern and learning to leap accurately between distant bass/chord positions.

Exercise 3.11 *Disc 1 Track #30*

In measures 10, 11 and 17 of *Exercise 3.12*, notice that the alternate bass is played at the beginning of the pattern.

Exercise 3.12 Disc 1 Track #31

Exercise 3.13 Disc 1 Track #32

The pattern in *Exercise 3.14* uses the alternate bass on the last beat of each measure instead of the third beat as in the previous exercises.

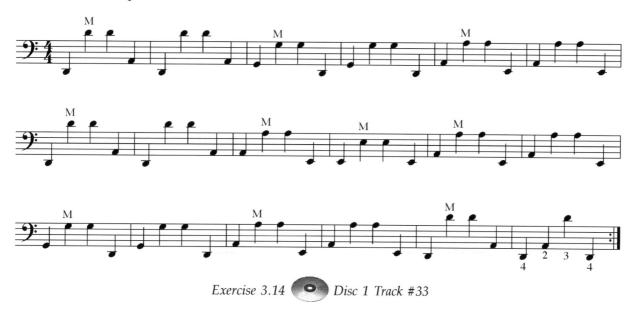

Exercise 3.14  Disc 1 Track #33

Exercise 3.15 presents patterns where some of the chords and alternate basses are played without the fundamental bass note. Be sure to use the correct fingerings.

Exercise 3.15 Disc 1 Track #34

There is a lot of movement in Exercise 3.16. You know the drill—play slowly at first, use the correct fingering, and learn it accurately.

Exercise 3.16  *Disc 1 Track #35*

Exercise 3.17 is loaded with challenges. Notice that the alternate bass and chord are played together in measure 3 and elsewhere. Measures 9, 10, 13 and 14 present leaps of considerable distance. Have fun!!

Exercise 3.17 Disc 1 Track #36

Ties

Notes of the same pitch can be combined to extend their time values. This is accomplished through the use of a TIE. A tie is indicated as a curved line connecting two notes of the same pitch. The second or tied note is not restruck, but held for the duration of the combined note values. In the example below, the note F would be struck once and played for the entire 8 beat total of the two whole notes.

In the example below, the tied half note and eighth note would be struck and played for a total duration of two and a half counts.

Rest

Silence in music is indicated by symbols on the staff called RESTS. Like notes, rests come in various time durations. A quarter note rest, for instance, gets one beat of silence. A half note rest gets two beats of silence. The example below shows the time duration of various rests.

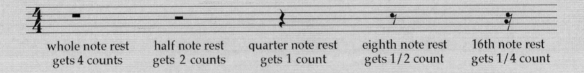

| whole note rest gets 4 counts | half note rest gets 2 counts | quarter note rest gets 1 count | eighth note rest gets 1/2 count | 16th note rest gets 1/4 count |

Accidentals

An ACCIDENTAL is a sharp (#), flat (b), double sharp (x), double flat (bb) or natural (♮) sign placed in front of a note to alter its pitch. Accidentals are shown when the note to be played is outside of the key signature. The alteration of the note by an accidental is valid only in the measure where it appears.

Minor Chords

Introducing the Minor Chord

The minor chord column is located next to the major chords as shown in *Illustration 4.1* (also refer to *Illustration 1.2* on page 12).

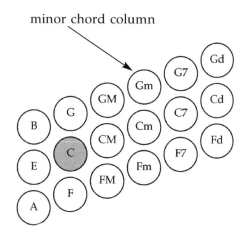

Illustration 4.1 – The minor chord column

To indicate the use of the minor chord, a lower case "m" is place above the note written on the staff. When playing a minor chord, use the fourth (ring) finger to play the fundamental bass and the second finger to play the minor chord. *Illustration 4.2* shows this convention.

Illustration 4.2

In *Exercise 4.1*, play both G major and G minor. Be careful to use the correct fingerings.

Exercise 4.1 *Disc 1 Track #37*

In *Exercises 4.2* through *4.4*, various combinations of major and minor chords are played. Practice slowly at first to develop accuracy of playing. Learn each exercise thoroughly before moving on to the next exercise.

Exercise 4.2 Disc 1 Track #38

Exercise 4.3 Disc 1 Track #39

Exercise 4.4 Disc 1 Track #40

The Minor Chord with Alternating Bass

Exercise 4.5 introduces the use of the alternating-bass pattern with the minor chord. The alternate bass is played with the third (middle) finger, maintaining the position of the fourth and second fingers on the fundamental bass and minor buttons respectively. Notice that measure 7 of *Exercise 4.5* uses the major chord and should be played with the proper fingering for the major pattern.

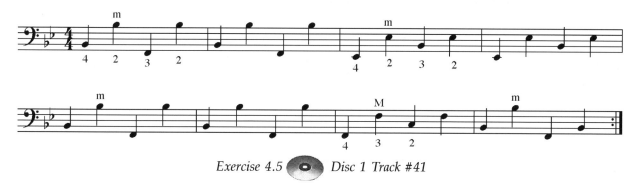

Exercise 4.5 Disc 1 Track #41

Exercise 4.6 uses both major and minor chords with alternating basses. Notice the "b" symbol in front of the E note in measure 13. This is called an accidental (see page 42), and it indicates that the Eb is to be played throughout the entire measure.

Exercise 4.6 Disc 1 Track #42

Exercise 4.7 and *Exercise 4.8* use minor and major chords with alternating basses, and will prove to be more challenging. Persevere—the reward of good playing is well worth it.

Exercise 4.7 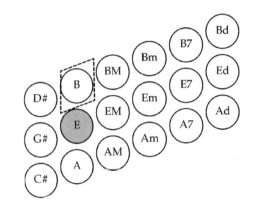 *Disc 1 Track #43*

Measure 4 of *Exercise 4.8* introduces the note B, the alternate bass of E. B is located above E, as shown in *Illustration 4.3* (also refer to *Illustration 1.2* on page 12).

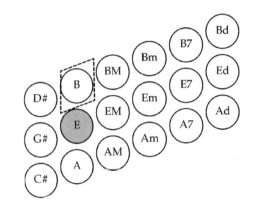

Illustration 4.3 – The note B lies above E

Exercise 4.8 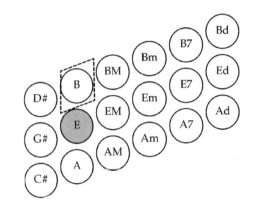 *Disc 1 Track #44*

More Fun with Minor Chords

Minor Chord Challenges

The final two exercises of this chapter are a bit more difficult. In *Exercise 4.9*, the bass and chord are sometimes played together, and the alternate bass is periodically used to start the alternating bass pattern.

Exercise 4.9 Disc 1 Track #45

In measures 7, 9, 21 and 23 of *Exercise 4.10*, the alternate bass pattern uses an alternative fingering from that which has previously been used.

Exercise 4.10 Disc 1 Track #46

This page has been left blank
to avoid awkward page turns.

Seventh Chords

Chapter 5

Introducing the Seventh Chord

The seventh chord column is located adjacent to the column of minor chords, as shown in *Illustration 5.1* (also refer to *Illustration 1.2* on page 12).

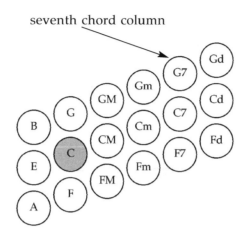

Illustration 5.1 – The seventh chord column

To notate the use of the seventh chord, a "7" is placed above the note written on the staff. When playing a seventh chord, use the fourth (ring) finger to play the fundamental bass and the second finger to play the seventh chord. *Exercise 5.1* shows this convention.

Exercise 5.1 Disc 2 Track #1

Exercise 5.2 uses the seventh chords.

Exercise 5.2 Disc 2 Track #2

Exercises 5.3 and *5.4* use the major, minor and seventh chords. Learn to play these exercises accurately before moving on to the next section.

Exercise 5.3   Disc 2 Track #3

Exercise 5.4   Disc 2 Track #4

The Seventh Chord with Alternating Bass

Exercise 5.5 introduces the use of the alternating-bass pattern with the seventh chord. Notice the alternate bass is played with the third (middle) finger, maintaining the position of the fourth and second fingers on the fundamental bass and seventh buttons respectively.

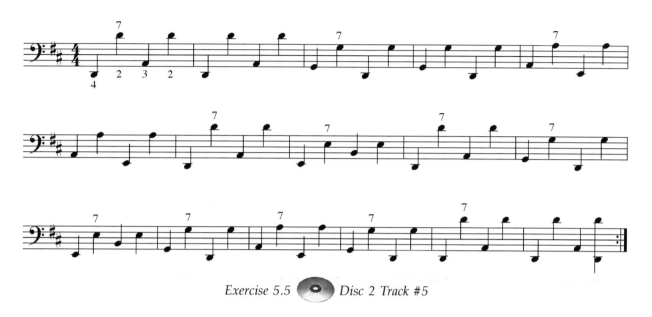

Exercise 5.5 Disc 2 Track #5

The following three exercises use major, minor and seventh chords with varying alternate bass patterns. In measure 3 of *Exercise 5.6*, B bass and B minor are used with their alternate bass F#, which is located above B (see *Illustration 1.2* on page 12). Be careful to follow the suggested fingerings.

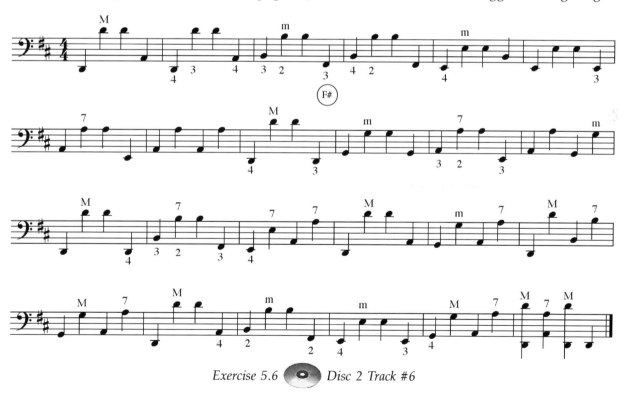

Exercise 5.6 Disc 2 Track #6

Exercise 5.7 Disc 2 Track #7

In *Exercises 5.8*, be sure to use the third finger on the alternate bass when played with the seventh chord.

Exercise 5.8 Disc 2 Track #8

Seventh Chords

A seventh chord is a major or minor triad plus the seventh degree above the root. Three common sevenths include the dominant, major and minor seven chords.

The DOMINANT SEVEN chord consists of a major triad plus a minor seventh above the root, as shown below. In accordion notation, the use of the dominant seven is indicated by placing a 7 over the note to be played. Notice that the abbreviation "dom" is typically not included with the chord name. In non-accordion notation, the dominant seven chord is typically notated with a 7 placed after the chord letter, as in C7.

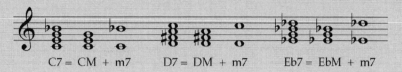

C7 = CM + m7   D7 = DM + m7   Eb7 = EbM + m7

A MAJOR SEVEN chord consists of a major triad plus a major seventh above the root, as illustrated below. A major seven is typically indicated by M7 or maj7, as in CM7 or Cmaj7.

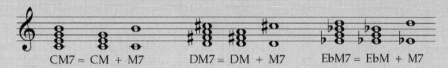

CM7 = CM + M7   DM7 = DM + M7   EbM7 = EbM + M7

A MINOR SEVEN chord consists of a minor triad plus a minor seventh interval, as shown. Use of the minor seven is indicated by a m7 or min7.

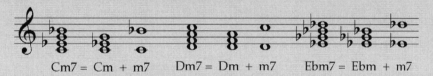

Cm7 = Cm + m7   Dm7 = Dm + m7   Ebm7 = Ebm + m7

This page has been left blank
to avoid awkward page turns.

The Counter Bass

Introducing the Counter Bass

The counter bass is the innermost column of the accordion's bass side, as shown in *Illustration 6.1* (also refer to *Illustration 1.2* on page 12). When playing a bass/chord pattern, use the fourth (ring) finger to play both the fundamental and the counter bass buttons.

The counter bass is the interval of a major third above the adjacent fundamental note. For example, if you are playing the bass note F, its related counter bass is A, which is the interval of a major third above F.

Exercise 6.1 introduces the use of the A counter bass in a pattern with the F bass note. To identify the use of the counter bass in written music, a short line is placed under the note.

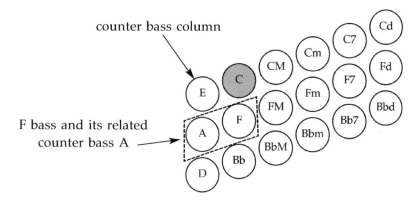

Illustration 6.1 – The counter bass column

Exercise 6.1 ◯ *Disc 2 Track #9*   This short line indicates the use of the counter bass.

The G in measure 1 of *Exercise 6.2* is the counter bass of Eb. Measure 2 introduces the Ab chord, which lies below Eb. The counter bass of Ab is C, as shown in *Illustration 6.2* (also refer to *Illustration 1.2* on page 12).

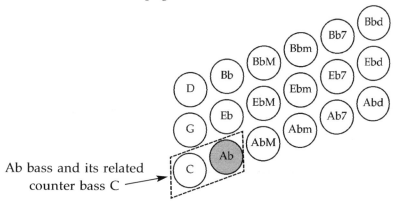

Illustration 6.2

On most accordions, the Ab bass note is physically marked with an indentation to assist in its identification.

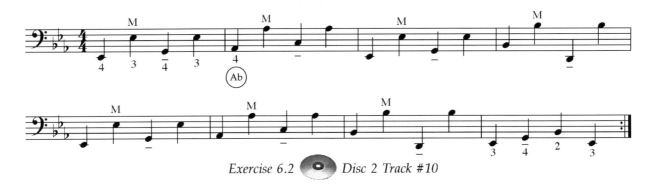

Exercise 6.2 Disc 2 Track #10

Exercise 6.3 uses both the counter bass and the alternate bass. In measure 5 the counter bass is used with the D7 chord.

Exercise 6.3 Disc 2 Track #11

Exercises 6.4 and *6.5* use the counter bass to create interesting bass movement. In *Exercise 6.4* be sure to use the suggested fingering in the final measure.

Exercise 6.4 Disc 2 Track #12

Be sure to use the suggested fingerings in *Exercise 6.5*.

Exercise 6.5   Disc 2 Track #13

Linear Bass Lines

With the use of the counter bass row, linear bass lines can be easily incorporated into bass patterns. A linear bass line is a series of adjacent notes which go up or down the staff. *Exercises 6.6* through *6.8* offer examples of how this can be achieved. In *Exercise 6.6*, the linear line is played with the bass notes A, G#, F#, E, D, C#, B and A.

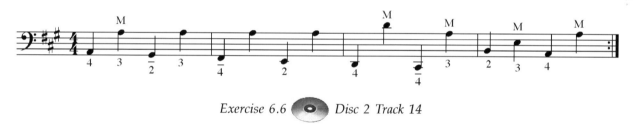

Exercise 6.6   Disc 2 Track 14

Notice the penultimate note in the final measure of *Exercise 6.7*. This note D is played with the same bass button as the D written one octave lower.

Exercise 6.7   Disc 2 Track #15

Notice the suggested fingerings in *Exercise 6.8*.

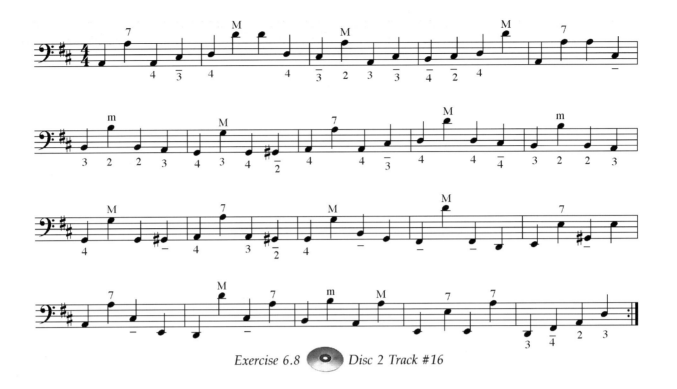

Exercise 6.8 💿 *Disc 2 Track #16*

Using the Fifth Finger

Exercises 6.9 through *6.12* introduce the use of the fifth (little) finger. As this is typically a weak finger, you may find these exercises difficult and awkward at first. Play slowly and practice them regularly to strengthen your fifth finger.

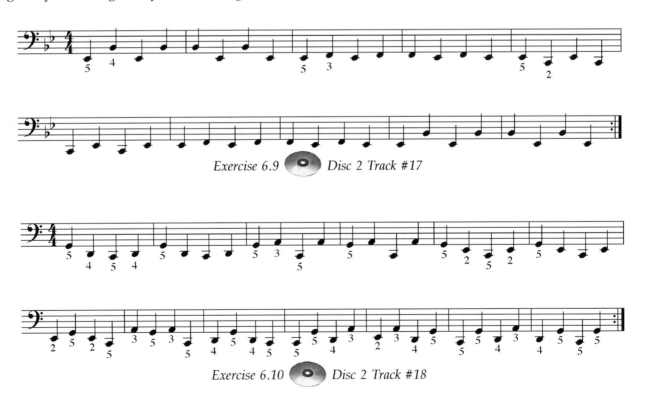

Exercise 6.9 💿 *Disc 2 Track #17*

Exercise 6.10 💿 *Disc 2 Track #18*

In *Exercises 6.11* and *6.12* be sure to use the indicated fingering.

Exercise 6.11 ⊙ *Disc 2 Track #19*

Exercise 6.12 ⊙ *Disc 2 Track #20*

Playing the Third with a Minor Chord

Exercises 6.13 through *6.16* use the interval of a minor third in a bass pattern with the minor chord. In *Exercises 6.13*, the minor third above C is Eb. Be sure you use the fifth finger as indicated to play the minor third.

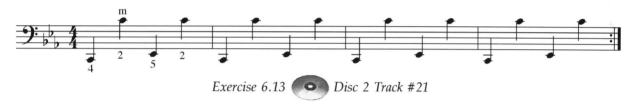

Exercise 6.13 ⊙ *Disc 2 Track #21*

Exercise 6.14 uses both the minor third and alternate bass with the minor chord.

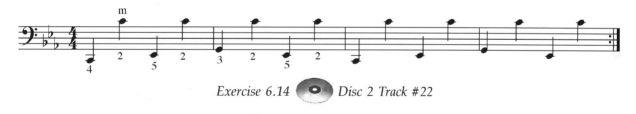

Exercise 6.14 ⊙ *Disc 2 Track #22*

The Db in measure 4 of *Exercise 6.15* is the minor third of Bb. Db lies below Ab (refer to *Illustration 1.2* on page 12).

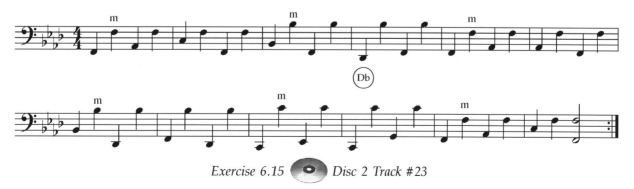

Exercise 6.15 ⊙ *Disc 2 Track #23*

Exercise 6.16 · Disc 2 Track #24

An Alternative Fingering

Exercise 6.17 introduces an alternative fingering. The C bass in measure 3 calls for the use of the third (middle) finger instead of the fourth finger. This may feel awkward at first. Practice slowly until it can be played comfortably and with accuracy.

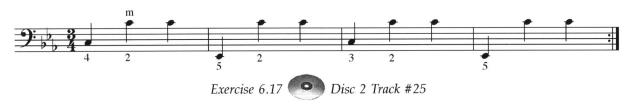

Exercise 6.17 · Disc 2 Track #25

Linear Bass Lines with Minor Chords

Exercise 6.18 incorporates a linear bass line with minor chords. Notice that the first note of each measure is a dotted half note. Be sure you play the note for its three beats throughout the entire measure. Use the correct fingering.

Exercise 6.18 · Disc 2 Track #26

Measure 5 of *Exercise 6.19* introduces the use of the third finger with the seventh chord. Playing the Ab in measure 6 may prove to be a challenging move. Be sure to keep your second finger close to the G7 at all times in that passage.

Exercise 6.19 • *Disc 2 Track #27*

Exercise 6.20 may be challenging at first. Practice slowly and persevere. Pay close attention to correct fingerings and the use of the alternate bass.

Exercise 6.20 • *Disc 2 Track #28*

This page has been left blank
to avoid awkward page turns.

Diminished Chords

Introducing the Diminished Chord

The diminished chord column is the outermost column of buttons on the accordion's bass side, as shown in *Illustration 7.1* (also refer to *Illustration 1.2* on page 12). In accordion notation, the diminished chord is identified by placing a lower case "d" over the note. When playing a diminished chord with its fundamental bass, use your fourth (ring) finger on the bass and the second finger on the diminished button.

diminished chord column

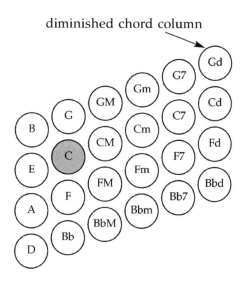

Illustration 7.1 – The diminished chord column

Practice *Exercises 7.1* and *7.2* slowly at first to develop accurate facility for playing the diminished chord.

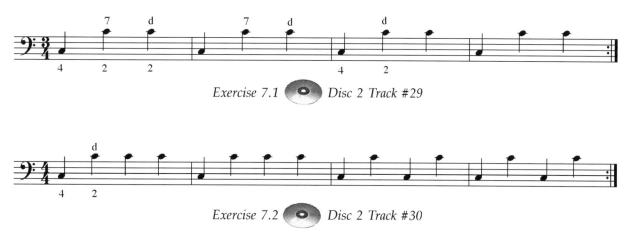

Exercise 7.1 Disc 2 Track #29

Exercise 7.2 Disc 2 Track #30

The leaps in the bass/diminished chord patterns get progressively greater in *Exercises 7.3* through *7.5*. Play slowly at first.

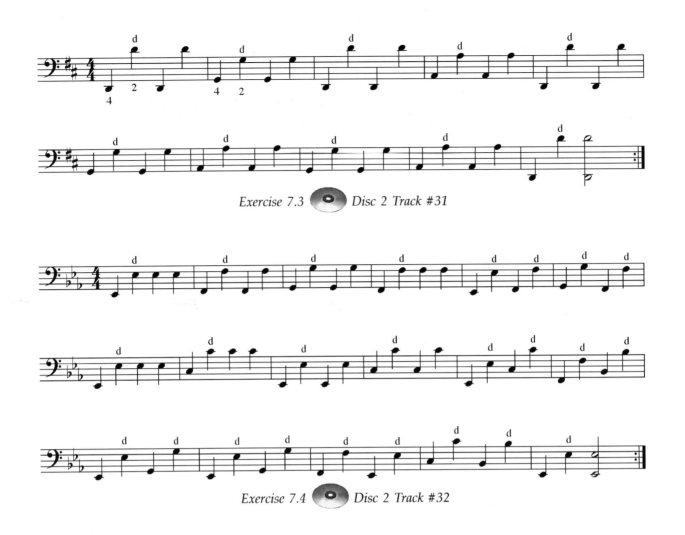

Exercise 7.3 Disc 2 Track #31

Exercise 7.4 Disc 2 Track #32

Exercise 7.5 may be challenging as there are long leaps between chords. Be careful to play F#, not F♮ in measure 5.

Exercise 7.5 Disc 2 Track #33

In *Exercise 7.6*, the diminished chord is used with other chords and bass patterns.

Exercise 7.6   *Disc 2 Track #34*

The Diminished Chord with Alternating Bass

Exercise 7.7 introduces the use of the alternate bass with the diminished chord. The alternate bass uses the interval of a diminished fifth (also referred to as b5). For example, the diminished fifth above Bb is Fb, which is the same sounding note as (the enharmonic equivalent of) E. When playing the Bb fundamental and Bb diminished chord, use the E (counter bass of C) as the alternate bass. *Illustration 7.2* illustrates the relationship.

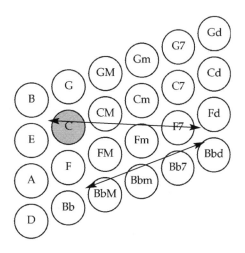

Illustration 7.2 – The fundamental bass, diminished chord and alternate bass

65

Exercise 7.7 will help you establish the fingering for the diminished/alternate bass pattern. Remember, Fb is the same note as E, and is the counter bass of C.

Exercise 7.7 🔘 Disc 2 Track #35

Exercises 7.8 and *7.9* use the diminished chord with the b5 alternate bass. Gb is enharmonic equivalent of F#, counter bass of D. Cb is the same note as B, counter bass of G.

Exercise 7.8 🔘 Disc 2 Track #36

Be sure to hold the dotted half notes for their full count value in *Exercise 7.9.*

Exercise 7.9 🔘 Disc 2 Track #37

The Diminished Chord with Linear Bass Lines

Exercises 7.10 through *7.13* incorporate linear bass lines with the diminished chord. The first eight measures of *Exercise 7.10* will help you establish the correct fingering position for the bass lines which follow.

Exercise 7.10   Disc 2 Track #38

In *Exercise 7.11*, the B♮ in measures 6, 14 and 15 is the same note as Cb, counter bass of G.

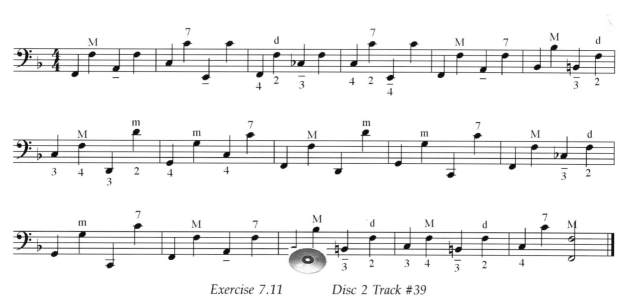

Exercise 7.11   Disc 2 Track #39

In measures 6, 10 and 15 of *Exercise 7.12*, the Bb is the enharmonic equivalent of A#, counter bass of F#.

Exercise 7.12   ◎   *Disc 2 Track #40*

Be careful to play the correct notes in *Exercise 7.13*. The Eb in measure 7 is the enharmonic equivalent of D#, counter bass of B. The Cb in measure 9 is the enharmonic equivalent of B, counter bass of G.

Exercise 7.13   ◎   *Disc 2 Track #41*

The Diminished Chord with the Sixth

Another pattern available with the diminished chord uses the interval of the major sixth.
For example, the major sixth above F is D. In measure 6 of *Example 7.14*, D counter bass of Bb is
used with the F diminished chord. *Exercises 7.14* and *7.15* use the major sixth in addition to the
alternating b5 bass with the diminished chord.

Exercise 7.14   *Disc 2 Track #42*

69

In measure 9 of *Exercise 7.15*, the D# is the counter bass of B. In measure 10, the F♮ is the same note as E#, counter bass of C#.

Exercise 7.15 💿 *Disc 2 Track #43*

Basic Music Theory

Diminished Chords

A DIMINISHED SEVEN chord (often referred to as diminished) consists of a diminished triad plus the interval of a diminished seventh, as shown below. There are several ways to write a chord symbol for the diminished seven chord—d, dim, dim7 or ⁰7.

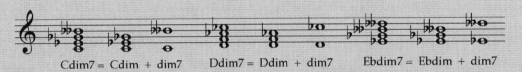

Cdim7 = Cdim + dim7   Ddim7 = Ddim + dim7   Ebdim7 = Ebdim + dim7

The interval of a diminished seventh over the note C is Bbb. Given that the notes Bbb and A have the same pitch, they are said to be an enharmonic equivalent. The same can be said for the notes Cb and B, as they are the same pitch.

The example below illustrates a second and more common spelling for the diminished chord.

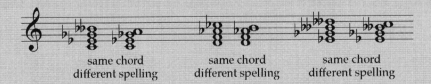

same chord   same chord   same chord
different spelling different spelling different spelling

Notice that the distance between any two adjacent notes in the diminished seven chord is a minor third (one and a half steps). The diminished seven chord is equidistant between all adjacent chord tones. Therefore, any chord tone can be the tonic or root of the chord. So for example, Cdim7 is C, Eb, Gb and A. Ebdim7 is Eb, Gb, Bbb (A) and C. Adim7 is A, C, Eb and Gb. The same notes make up all of these chords.

The Half Diminished Chord

The half diminished seven chord is made by combining a diminished triad (root, minor third and diminished fifth) with a minor seventh interval. The C half diminished seven, for example, is made with the notes C, Eb, Gb and Bb.

Compare this to a C diminished seven, made of the notes C, Eb, Gb and A and notice that the difference is the fourth note—Bb vs. A. See *Illustration 7.3* below.

The symbol for a half diminished chord is ø.

$C^{ø}$= C Eb Gb Bb   Cdim = C Eb Gb A

Illustration 7.3 – The half diminished and diminished seven chords

Notice that the top three notes of the C half diminished chord (Eb, Gb and Bb) make an Eb minor chord.

The C bass note can be combined with the Eb minor chord button to create a C half diminished chord.

Both the C bass and C counter bass of Ab are available to play in combination with the Eb minor button, as shown in *Illustration 7.4*.

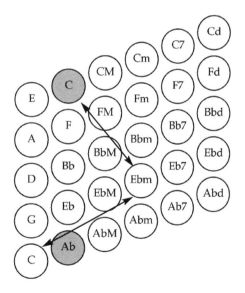

Illustration 7.4 – C half diminished

The C counter bass of Ab and Eb minor button is the easier combination to play. There are four fingering options available to play this combination, as shown in *Illustration 7.5*.

Illustration 7.5 – C half diminished fingering with the C counter bass note

The C bass and Eb minor button combination has two practical fingering options, as shown in *Illustration 7.6*.

Illustration 7.6 – C half diminished fingering with the C bass note

In *Exercise 7.16*, the C minor is used to prepare your hand for the Aø. In this case, the A is taken from the counter bass of F position.

Exercise 7.16   *Disc 2 Track #44*

In *Exercise 7.17*, the fifth finger is sometimes used to play the counter bass notes.

Exercise 7.17   *Disc 2 Track #45*

Exercise 7.18 uses both the diminished and half diminished chords. Pay attention to the suggested fingerings. Be sure to keep your second finger on the Em button when making the transition from the Em to C#ø positions in measures 6 and 7. The Bb in measure 10 is the enharmonic equivalent of A# and is the counter bass of nearby F#. In measure 12, the Ab is the same as G#, counter bass of E.

Exercise 7.18   Disc 2 Track #46

Exercise 7.19 uses the G half diminished chord played with the G bass note and the Bb minor chord button.

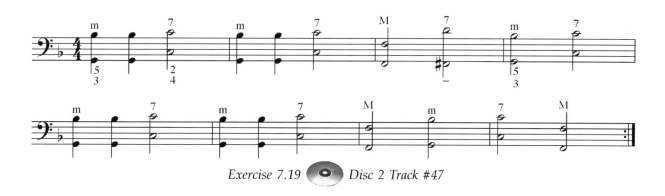

Exercise 7.19   Disc 2 Track #47

73

Advanced Techniques

Chord Combinations

Dominant, Major and Minor Seven Chords

Overview

All of the exercises encountered in this book thus far have been limited to playing only one chord button at a time—the major, minor, seventh or diminished. But in our musical lexicon, there are numerous other chords, including major and minor sevenths, sixths, ninths, elevenths, minor seven flat fives, and the list goes on and on.

Though it is not possible to play most of these chords by pressing only one button, two chord buttons can be played simultaneously to vastly increase the accordion's chordal repertoire. The following chapters introduce new chords and present exercises with advanced chord progressions using chord button combinations.

To add clarity and assist in identifying the chords, the chord names will now be included above the staff in the exercises.

One Button—Three Notes

Every chord button on the accordion plays three and only three distinct notes. This is obvious for the C major button, which plays C, E and G. Likewise, C minor is sounded by playing the notes C, Eb and G. But a full C7 chord includes the notes C, E, G and Bb. Does the accordion's C7 button play all four of these notes?

No, it does not. It plays only three, leaving out the fifth of the chord—the note G.

What about the diminished button? The full C diminished seven chord includes the notes C, Eb, Gb and A. But the diminished button leaves out the flatted fifth. Hence, the C diminished button plays the notes C, Eb and A.

As it turns out, this simplification of the accordion's bass mechanism allows for the successful use of button combinations in creating chords not otherwise available to the bass side.

Of course it must be stated that there is the option of creating chords by combining notes played on the accordion's keyboard side with the bass buttons. This technique will not be covered in this volume.

Notating Chord Combinations

When notating a chord combination, the chord quality symbols are place over the notes on the staff in the same order as the notes themselves. The example below calls for the G diminished and C major buttons to be played together. Notice the note G is located below the C, hence the symbol "d" indicating use of the G diminished is located below the "M", which indicates use of the C major.

The same holds true for the fingering suggestions. The "2" in the above example indicates use of the second (index) finger on the G diminished button, while the "3" (middle finger) is used on the C major.

The Full Dominant Seven Chord

A full four note dominant seven chord consists of the root, major third, perfect fifth and minor seventh (see page 53 for discussion of seventh chords). There are a number of button combinations involving the use of C, C7 and/or Gdim available to play a full four note chord.

The C7 button plays the notes C, E and Bb.

The C major button plays the notes C, E and G.

Pressing the C major and C seventh buttons together plays the notes C, E, G and Bb.

This combination with the C bass can be played using your second, third and fourth fingers.

The G diminished button plays the notes G, Bb and E.

Pressing the C major and G diminished buttons together plays the notes C, E, G and Bb.

C7 = C E G Bb

There are two fingering options available to create an accompaniment pattern involving the CM/Gdim combination with the C bass.

And finally, pressing the C seventh and G diminished buttons together also plays the full four note C7 chord.

C7 = C E G Bb

There are two fingering options for this combination with the C bass.

It should also be noted that another option for playing a C7 chord is to press the G diminished button. This plays the notes E, G and Bb—three of the four chord tones.

There are two fingering options for playing the Gdim with a C bass.

Exercises 8.1 through *8.6* use the chord combinations discussed above to create full four note seven chords. For clarity, notice that the chord names are now included in the exercises.

Exercise 8.1

Exercise 8.2

In *Exercise 8.3* the major and seventh chord combination is played with a bass note.

Exercise 8.3

Exercise 8.4 uses the major/diminished chord combination to create a dominant seven.

Exercise 8.4

The bluesy pattern of *Exercise 8.5* uses the seventh and diminished chord combination and presents a healthy challenge to the fifth finger.

Exercise 8.5

Exercise 8.6 uses both the major/diminished and the seventh/diminished combinations. Play the exercise with a syncopated eighth note feel.

Exercise 8.6

The Minor Seven Chord

The minor seven chord includes the root with the intervals of a minor third, perfect fifth and minor seven. The notes which make up a C minor seven chord, for example, include C, Eb, G and Bb.

Notice that the first three notes of the chord can be played with the C minor bass button.

Cm = C Eb G

The top three notes of the C minor seven chord—Eb, G and Bb—are the notes of the Eb major button.

EbM = Eb G Bb

Combining the C minor and Eb major buttons plays all the notes of a C minor seven.

Cm7 = C Eb G Bb

There are two bass/chord combination positions convenient for playing a minor seven chord. The first uses the root of the chord from the fundamental column. Using C as an example, play the C bass in the fundamental column in combination with the Eb major button. There are two fingering options. Notice that in this combination, the note C is left out of the chord.

The C minor button can easily be added to create a four note minor seven chord.

The second position available to create a minor seven chord plays the root of the chord in the counter bass column. In this case the C, counter bass of Ab, is used with the Eb major chord. There are three fingering options available to play this combination.

Exercises 8.7 through *Exercise 8.13* present examples of minor seven chords with varying chord patterns. Both the fundamental and counter bass positions are used.

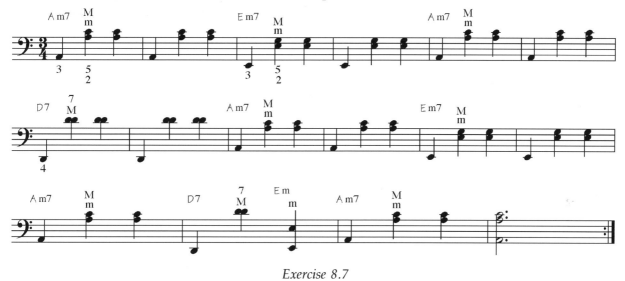

Exercise 8.7

Like the above exercise, *Exercises 8.8* through *8.10* use the root of the chord from the fundamental column in combination with chord buttons to create the minor seven.

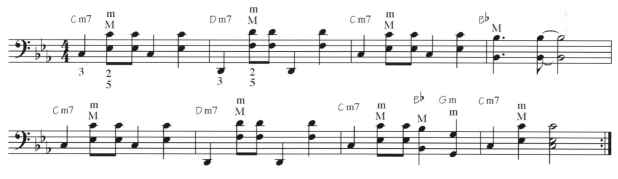

Exercise 8.8

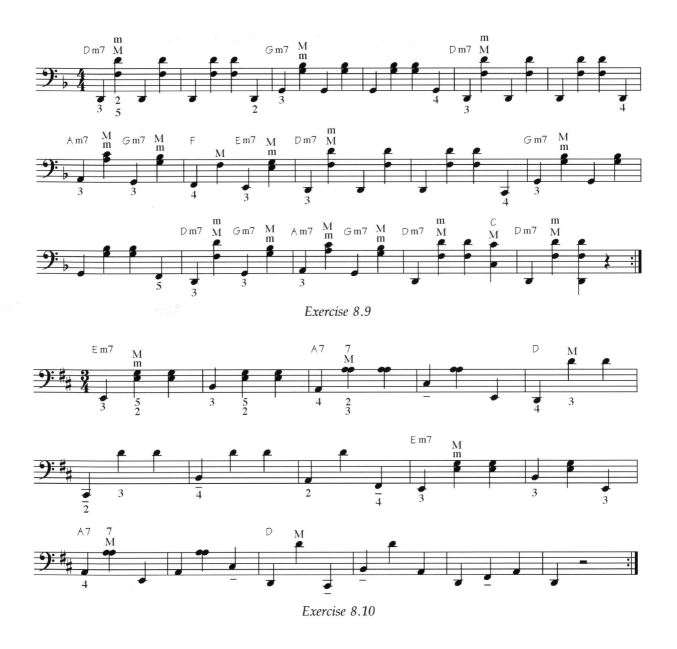

Exercise 8.9

Exercise 8.10

Exercise 8.11 takes the root of the chord from the counter bass position.

Exercise 8.11

Exercise 8.12 uses the root from the counter bass played at the same time as the chord to create a nice sounding minor seven chord progression.

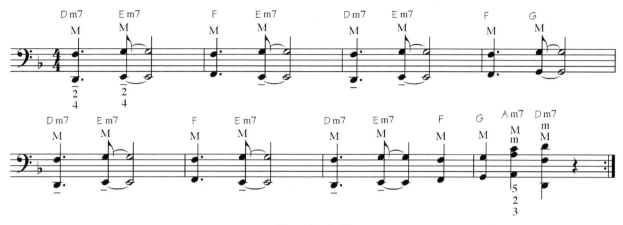

Exercise 8.12

In *Exercise 8.13*, linear bass lines are played with the minor seven chord. Notice that both the fundamental and counter bass positions are used. The Gb in measure 2 is the enharmonic equivalent of F#, counter bass of D. The Gb in measure 10 is located below Db (refer to *Illustration 1.2* on page 12).

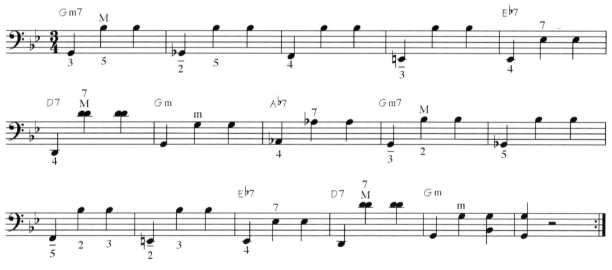

Exercise 8.13

The Major Seven Chord

The major seven chord includes the root, major third, perfect fifth and major seven.
C major seven, for example, is played with the notes C, E, G and B. Notice that the top three notes of the chord can be played by pressing the E minor button.

Em = E   G   B

Combining the C major and the E minor buttons creates the four note major seven chord.

CM7 = C   E   G   B

The example shown above, though, is quite awkward to reach when used with the C bass note, and for all practical purposes is not very useful. Consequently the position used here to play the major seven chord will include the bass note and only the related minor chord button, played with the fifth and second fingers, respectively.

Exercises 8.14 through *8.18* use the major seven position with other chord combinations.

Exercise 8.14

Exercise 8.15

84

In *Exercise 8.16*, the well known ii–V–I chord progression is used (see next page for a discussion of chord symbols). You can now play the ii as a minor seven, the V as a dominant seven and the I as a major seven.

Exercise 8.16

In *Exercise 8.17* the chord combinations creating the major and minor seven chords are played together with the root, third and alternate bass notes. Variations of the ii–V–I chord progression are used.

Exercise 8.17

Notice that the D notes in measures 4 and 5 of *Exercise 8.18* are played in different positions. The D of measure 4 is played as the counter bass of Bb, while the D of measure 5 is played in the fundamental column.

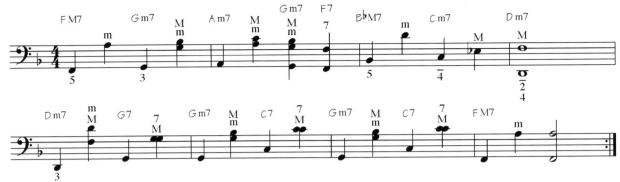

Exercise 8.18

Basic Music Theory

Chord Nomenclature

Chords in a key can be assigned numbers, and chord progressions can be described using those numbers. The advantage of this system is that it is key independent.

Let's build seventh chords on each degree of a C major scale, using only notes in that scale.

We can assign a number to each chord sequentially from C, using Roman numerals. Additionally, if the chord is major, we'll use an upper case number. If the chord is minor, we'll use a lower case. When we analyze the C scale, here's what we get:

I – C major seven
ii – D minor seven
iii – E minor seven
IV – F major seven
V – G dominant seven
vi – A minor seven
vii – B minor seven b5

We can build chords over the scale tones of any major key, as above. Though the chord names will change for any scale degree, the chord quality stays the same. Hence, the I chord in any major key is a major chord. The ii chord is always minor, the iii chord always minor, the IV always major, etc.

We now have a convenient way to refer to chord changes. For a ii–V–I chord change in the key of C, play Dm–G–C. In the key of G it becomes Am–D–G.

We can notate seventh chords by writing $ii^{m7} – V^7 – I^{M7}$. In the key of D, this would be Em7–A7–DM7.

The m7(b5) – 7(b9) Progression

The 7(b9) Chord

A common minor key chord progression found in jazz tunes is $ii^{m7(b5)} - V^{7(b9)} - i^{m7}$ ($A^{m7(b5)} - D^{7(b9)} - G^{m7}$ for example). This progression can be played on the accordion's bass.

The 7(b9) chord is a dominant seven chord plus the interval of a flatted ninth. A G7(b9) for example (shown below in both the treble and bass clefs) includes the notes G, B, D, F and Ab.

G dominant 7 b9   B dim   G dominant 7 b9   B dim

Notice that the top four notes of the chord—B, D, F and Ab—are the notes making up a diminished seven chord. Remember that any note of a diminished seven chord can be the root of the chord (see page 70), and that the accordion's diminished button plays only three of the four notes of the chord, omitting the b5. Therefore the B, F and Ab diminished buttons are available in combination with the G bass note to create a G7(b9). (The D diminished button is not an option because it omits the Ab note, which is the b9.) Given the location of the note G, in either the fundamental or counter bass positions, the F and Ab diminished buttons are the only practical choices.

Using the G in the fundamental position, there are several options available to create a G7(b9). The first is to play the G bass with the F diminished button. There are two fingerings convenient for this position.

The F diminished button plays the notes D, F and Ab, leaving out B, the major third of G7(b9). Either the G major or G seventh buttons can be combined with the F diminished to create the full chord. These positions may feel awkward at first and take some practice to get used to.

87

The G7(b9) can also be played from the counter bass position. G counter bass of Eb can be combined with the Ab diminished button, which plays the notes Ab, B and F. Notice that D, the fifth of the chord is missing in this combination. Two fingerings are convenient for this position.

Exercise 9.1 introduces the major/diminished combination to play the 7(b9). The major chord is played first to help establish the correct fingering for the combination.

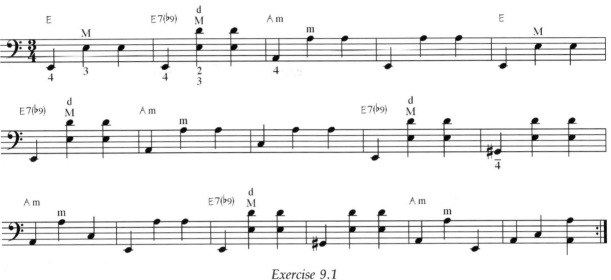

Exercise 9.1

Exercise 9.2 again uses the major/diminished combination.

Exercise 9.2

In *Exercise 9.3* the seventh/diminished combination is used to create the 7(b9). The exercise starts out with the seventh chord alone to help establish the correct position.

Exercise 9.3

Exercise 9.4 uses the seventh/diminished combination played together with the bass note.

Exercise 9.4

Exercise 9.5 uses the counter bass position to play the m7(b9) chord. The Bb diminished is played first to assist in finding the proper position.

Exercise 9.5

Exercise 9.6 incorporates moving bass lines with the m7(b9) chord. Use the indicated fingerings and be sure to notice whether the bass note is played in the fundamental or counter bass column. This exercise may prove to be a bit of challenge.

Exercise 9.6

The m7(b5) Chord

The m7(b5) is a minor seven chord with the fifth flatted by a half step. For example, an Em7 is made of the notes E, G, B and D. An Em7(b5) is E, G, Bb and D. Shown below are the chords in both the treble and bass clefs.

Notice that G, Bb and D are the notes which make a G minor chord. The E bass can be played with the G minor chord button to create a Gm7(b5).

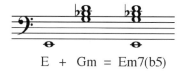

Playing only the G minor button however leaves out the note E. To create a four note chord, the G minor can be combined with the G diminished button, sounding all the notes of the m7(b5).

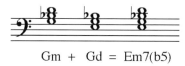

The most practical fingering for the m7(b5) uses the counter bass with either the minor or the minor/diminished combination. For example, E counter bass of C can be played with G minor or the combination of G minor and G diminished.

There are various finger combinations available to play E counter bass with G minor.

There are two practical fingering options for the counter bass with the minor/diminished combination.

The E bass note can also be played in the fundamental position with the G minor chord to create an Em7(b5). There are various fingerings available to play this combination. Note however that it is not practical to play the E bass in the fundamental column with the G minor/diminished combination.

SPECIAL NOTE—The m7(b5) and m6 Chords

The m7(b5) chord is also referred to by two other common names. The notes which make a Em7(b5) for example (E, G, Bb and D) are also the same notes of the Gm6 chord and Gm/E (G minor with an E in the bass). These chords are shown below in the treble clef.

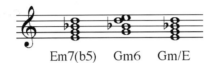

Em7(b5)   Gm6   Gm/E

Exercise 9.7 introduces the m7(b5) played in the counter bass position. G bass to Gm is first played to help establish the correct position. The E counter bass is then played with the G minor chord.

Exercise 9.7

Exercise 9.8 introduces the ii$^{m7(b5)}$ – V$^{7(b9)}$ chord progression.

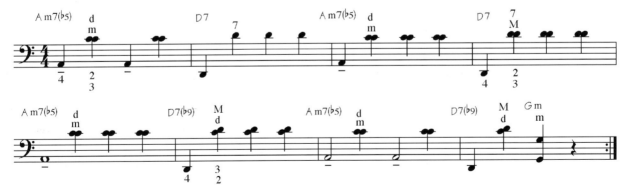

Exercise 9.8

92

In *Exercise 9.9* the root of the m7(b5) chord is played in the counter bass position using the fifth finger.

Exercise 9.9

Exercise 9.10 offers four variations on the ii$^{\text{m7(b5)}}$ – V$^{7\text{(b9)}}$ – i$^{\text{m7}}$ chord progression. Pay attention to the use of counter bass and fundamental positions.

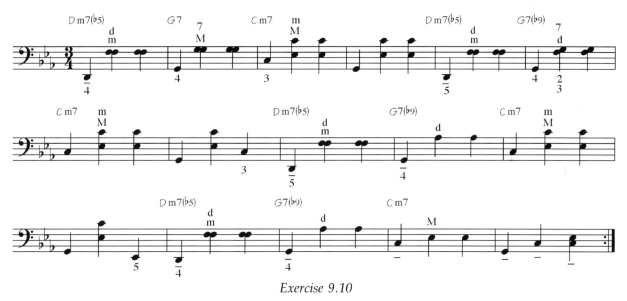

Exercise 9.10

Exercise 9.11 uses the fundamental bass with the m7(b5) chord. Play the repetitive G minor with indicated fingerings to assist in finding the correct position.

Exercise 9.11

93

In *Exercise 9.12* the Em7(b5) is played in the fundamental position to execute the ii^{m7(b5)} – V^{7(b9)} – i^{m7} chord progression.

Exercise 9.12

The Major and Minor Six Chords

Introducing the Major Six Chord

The major six chord consists of a major triad plus the interval of a major sixth above the root. A C6 for example (shown below in both the treble and bass clefs) includes the notes C, E, G and A.

CM + M6 = C6   CM + M6 = C6

There are two options for playing a C6 on the accordion's bass side. The first uses the C bass note with the A minor chord. There are two fingerings convenient for this position, as shown below. Notice that this combination is missing G, the fifth of the chord.

C + Am = C + A, C, E = C6

C6

5   2   4   2

A full C6 chord can be created by combining the C major and the Am minor buttons. The fingering for this position is shown below.

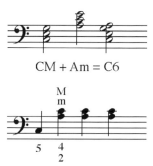

CM + Am = C6

M
m

5   4
2

Exercise 10.1 uses the single minor bass button, three–note version of the major six chord. Practice using both the fourth and fifth fingers (shown in parenthesis) on the fundamental bass notes as indicated.

95

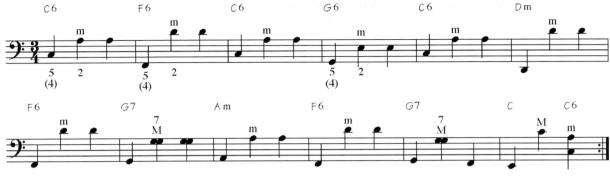

Exercise 10.1

In *Exercise 10.2*, the full major six chord is created by use of chord combinations.

Exercise 10.2

Notice the fingering changes in measures 9 and 12 of *Exercise 10.3* to facilitate the use of the alternate bass.

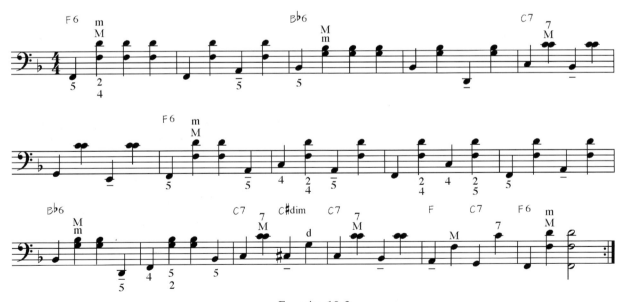

Exercise 10.3

Exercise 10.4 uses the major six with some common chord progressions. The C natural in measure 3 should be played as the counter bass of G#.

Exercise 10.4

Exercise 10.5 may offer a bit of a challenge. Pay attention to the suggested fingerings. Notice the use of the m7(b5) and 7(b9) chords.

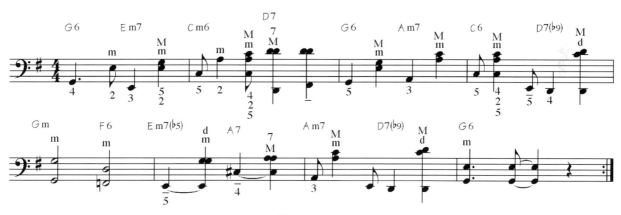

Exercise 10.5

Introducing the Minor Six Chord

The minor six chord consists of a minor triad plus the interval of a major sixth above the root. A Cm6 for example (shown below in both the treble and bass clefs) includes the notes C, Eb, G and A.

Cm + M6 = Cm6

Cm + M6 = Cm6

The Cm6 can be created on the accordion by combining the C minor and the C diminished buttons. (Remember, the C diminished button plays only three notes—C, Eb and A.) The fingering position for this chord is shown below.

Cm + Cdim = Cm6

Notice the Cm6 chord comprises the same notes as the Am7(b5)—A, C, Eb and G (see page 92). When playing the Am7(b5), combine the C minor and C diminished buttons as in the Cm6, but use the bass note A (counter bass of F), not C.

Exercises 10.6 and *10.7* introduce the use of the minor six chord.

Exercise 10.6

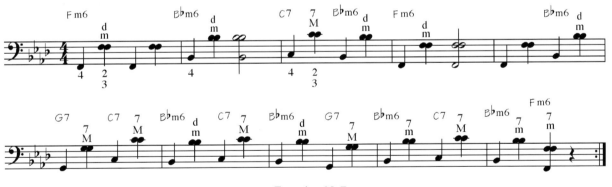

Exercise 10.7

Exercise 10.8 uses both the minor six and major six chords. The Ab in measure seven is the enharmonic equivalent of G# and is played as the counter bass of E. The Gb of measure eight is the enharmonic equivalent of F#, counter bass of D.

Exercise 10.8

Exercise 10.9 presents four variations of the ii–V–i chord progression using the minor six chord. Notice in measure 3 that the Bbm6 uses the same chord combination as the Gm7(b5). Only the bass note changes—from Bb to G. Notice also that in measure 3 the second finger is used to play the Bb diminished button. Keep that finger in place as you change to the C7(b9) chord of measure 4, as that diminished button is used for both the Gm7(b5) and the C7(b9) chords. Keeping your second finger in place will facilitate making the chord change accurately.

Exercise 10.9

Exercise 10.10 introduces the minor seven to minor six chord change. Play the F♮ of measure 11 as the counter bass of C#.

Exercise 10.10

Major, Dominant and Minor Nine Chords

Chapter 11

Introducing the Major Nine Chord

An easy way to understand the major nine chord is to see it as two major chords stacked on top of each other. For example, a CM9 consists of the notes C, E, G, B and D.

CM9 = C E G B D

Notice that the first three notes make a C major chord. And notice that the last three notes make a G major chord. Consequently, we can think of a CM9 as a CM plus GM, as shown below in both the treble and bass clefs.

CM + GM = CM9

CM + GM = CM9

A major nine chord is easily played on the basses by combining two adjacent major chord buttons. CM9 for example is played by combining the CM and GM buttons.

C GM + CM = CM9

The fingering for this combination is shown below.

One other chord combination can be made to play the CM9. Combining the GM and Em buttons along with the C bass note creates a CM9.

C Em + GM = CM9

C Em + GM = CM9

101

The fingering for this chord combination is somewhat awkward.

Exercise 11.1 introduces the use of the major nine chord.

Exercise 11.1

In Exercise *11.2*, notice the similarity between the GM9 of measures two and six, and the Bm7 of measure six.

Exercise 11.2

Be sure to notice the use of the M9 and the M6 chords in *Exercise 11.3*. Keep your second finger on the D minor button when changing from the Dm7 to the F6 in measures 4 and 5.

Exercise 11.3

Exercise 11.4 uses alternating and counter basses with the major nine chord. Pay attention to the suggested fingerings.

Exercise 11.4

The Dominant Nine Chord

Similar to the major nine chord, the dominant nine chord can be viewed as two chords stacked on top of one another. For example, C dominant nine—notated as C9— includes the notes C, E G, Bb and D as shown below.

C9 = C E G Bb D

The first three notes of the C9 chord (C, E, G) are a C major chord. The top three notes (G, Bb, D) are a G minor chord. Thus, a C9 is a combination of C major and G minor, as shown below in the treble and bass clefs.

CM + Gm = C9

CM + Gm = C9

On the accordion's bass, the C9 is made by pressing a combination of the C major and G minor buttons.

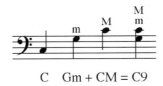

C   Gm + CM = C9

There are two options for fingering this combination.

A C9 chord can also be made by combining a C7 chord (C, E, G, Bb) with a G minor chord (G, Bb, D). Remember that the accordion plays only three notes per chord button, consequently the C7 button plays the notes C, E and Bb.

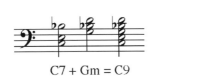

C7 + Gm = C9

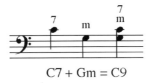

C7 + Gm = C9

There are two fingering options for this somewhat awkward combination.

One other combination which creates a C9 chord includes the C bass note with the G minor chord (G, Bb, D) and the G diminished chord (G, Bb, Db, E). Again, because the accordion plays only three note chords, the Db of the G diminished chord is not included when pressing the G diminished button.

C   Gm+ Gd = C9   C   Gm+ Gd = C9

There are two fingering options for this combination.

Exercise 11.5 introduces the use of the dominant nine chord.

Exercise 11.5

Exercise 11.6 uses the dominant nine chord in a ii–V–I chord progression. When changing from the Em7 chord combination to the A9 combination, as in measures 1 and 2, be sure to keep your second finger on the Em button. This will assist in making the change accurately. In measure 8, notice the use of the minor/diminished combination to create the A9 chord. An alternative fingering is used in measure 9 to facilitate the bass note movement.

Exercise 11.6

Exercise 11.7 uses a Dm7(b5) to G9 chord progression. Notice that D counter bass of Bb is used in measure 5, while D bass is used in measure 7.

Exercise 11.7

The Minor Nine Chord

The minor nine chord is made by playing the chord root, minor third, perfect fifth, minor seventh and major ninth above the root. C minor nine, for example, consists of the notes C, Eb, G, Bb and D, as shown below.

C Eb G Bb D = Cm9

The minor nine chord can be seen as two chords stacked on each other. The lower three notes of a Cm9 make a C minor chord, while the top three notes make a G minor chord. These are shown below in both the treble and bass clefs.

Cm + Gm = Cm9   Cm + Gm = Cm9

On the accordion, the C minor and the G minor bass buttons can be played together to produce this chord combination.

C   Gm + Cm = Cm9

Two fingering options for this combination are shown below.

One other combination is available to make a Cm9. The C note can be combined with an Eb major and G minor chord, as shown below.

C   EbM + Gm = Cm9

This combination can be played on the accordion bass using the EbM and the Gm buttons.

C   EbM + Gm = Cm9

The fingering for this combination is awkward.

Exercise 11.8 juxtaposes the minor nine, major nine and dominant nine chords.

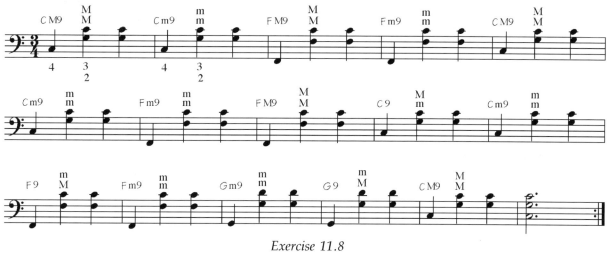

Exercise 11.8

Exercise 11.9 uses the minor nine in the context of a ii–V–I progression.

Exercise 11.9

Exercise 11.10 uses the m7, m7(b5) and m9 as ii chords in various ii–V–I progressions. Notice the use of C counter bass of Ab in measure 5.

Exercise 11.10

The Leftovers

This final chapter will offer a cursory overview of four common chords not covered in previous chapters. Unfortunately none of the chords—the augmented triad, the six/nine chord, the minor major seven chord and the suspended four chord—can be played accurately on the accordion's bass. As you will see, the chords can be approximated by playing chord button combinations which include additional notes.

The Augmented Triad

The augmented triad consists of the root, major third and augmented fifth. For example, C augmented fifth (usually shown as Caug or C+5) includes the notes C, E and G#.

C E G# = Caug

There is no chord button or chord combination that can create an augmented chord on the accordion's bass. Furthermore, playing the major chord button in place of the augmented chord will cause a clash if the augmented fifth is being played on the right hand or by another player. For example, the G note of a C major chord will clash with the G# of a C augmented chord.

One work–around to this conflict is to play the seventh chord button, as the fifth is omitted (the C7 button plays only the notes C, E and Bb). But be aware, use of the dominant seven chord will not always be appropriate.

One button combination that can provide an augmented fifth is the tonic played as a bass note, plus the major chord of the third. For example, C bass note plus E major plays the notes C, E, G# and B.

C + EM = CM7(+5)

The problem here is the addition of the major seven—in this case the note B—which is likely to be inappropriate to the musical setting. The fingering for this combination is shown below.

The Six/Nine Chord

The six/nine chord (also sometimes called the six add nine chord) is a major six chord plus the interval of a major ninth. C6/9 for example includes the notes C, E, G, A and D.

C   E   G   A   D = C6/9

There is no button or bass combination that can create a six/nine chord on the accordion. If use of the seventh is acceptable, there are two possible chords that include the 6/9—the M9(add6) and the 9(add6)

The CM9(add6) includes the notes C, E, G, A, B and D. Notice the addition of the major seventh (B) to the 6/9.

C   E   G   A   B   D = CM9add6

The M9(add6) can be played on the bass by using a three button combination. CM9(add6) for example, can be played by combining the CM, GM and Am buttons.

CM + GM + Am = CM9(add6)

The fingering for this combination is shown below.

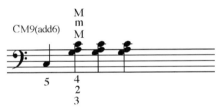

One other chord combination is available to create a six/nine chord, but it includes the dominant seventh, which may not be appropriate to the musical setting. The C9add6 includes the notes C, E, G, A, Bb and D. Notice the addition of the dominant seventh (Bb) to the 6/9.

C   E   G   A   Bb   D = C9(add6)

The 9(add6) can be played by combining three buttons. To play C9(add6) for example, combine the CM, Gm and Am buttons.

CM + Gm + Am = C9(add6)

This combination can be played with the following fingering.

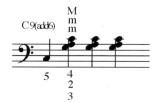

The Minor Major Seven Chord

The minor major seven chord is made by combining a minor triad plus a major seventh. CmMaj7 for example includes the notes C, Eb, G and B.

C Eb G B = CmMaj7

There is no button combination that can create this chord. If the addition of the ninth is acceptable to the setting, the mMaj9 can be substituted. CmMaj9 for example includes the notes C, Eb, G, B and D.

C Eb G B D = CmMaj9

This can be played by combining the C minor plus the G major.

Cm + GM = CmMaj9

The combination can be played with the following fingering.

The Suspended Four Chord

The suspended four (usually shown as sus4) is made by playing the chord root, the perfect fourth and the perfect fifth. Csus4 for example includes the notes C, F and G.

C F G = Csus4

There is no button combination that can play only these notes. If the addition of the major sixth is acceptable, the tonic can be played with the major chord of the fourth.

For example, C bass button and F major can be combined to play the notes C, F and A, providing the suspended fourth (F) plus the major sixth (A).

C FM = C6sus4

There are two easy fingering for this combination as shown below.

Note that the sus4 typically resolves to the major triad. Hence a Csus4 (or the C6sus4) resolves to C major.

54378557R00064

Made in the USA
San Bernardino,
CA